Religion, Nationalism and Eco

Matthew Schoffeleers
Daniel Meijers

Religion, Nationalism and Economic Action
Critical questions on Durkheim and Weber

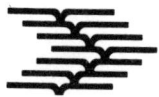

1978
VAN GORCUM, Assen, The Netherlands

© 1978 Van Gorcum & Comp. B.V., P.O.Box 43, 9400 AA Assen, the Netherlands

No parts of this book may be reproduced in any form, by print, photoprint, microfilm or any other means without written permission from the publishers.

ISBN 90 232 1614 8

Printed in The Netherlands by Van Gorcum, Assen

Preface

Morality is not a popular subject among sociologists, who seem happy to leave it to the philosophers and the theologians. There was a time, though, when things were different and morality stood in the forefront of sociological interest. One need only think of Weber and Durkheim. Weber's most influential work was on morality as a determining influence on man's economic behaviour, and Durkheim saw it as his life-long vocation to develop a sociological theory of morality which could serve as the basis of a behavioural code for modern man. Their respective influence however has been quite divergent. Weber's thesis on the Protestant ethic has inspired a long and often lively debate, in which historians and economists joined ranks with the sociologists. Durkheim's writings on morality never aroused that kind of wide-spread theoretical interest despite the fact that they deal with issues of vital concern to present-day societies. One of those issues is the role of the nation in the modern world, which is the subject of the first of the two essays in this volume.

For Durkheim, the nation was a mode of human sociation which could play an integrating role in the modern world. It embodied the idea of continuity as it was the repository of a formal history. It could inspire a sense of pride and of belonging in terms of that history. Finally, it provided a setting within which individuals could identify objectives in life. Briefly, the nation was to be more than a collection of groups, sub-groups and individuals; it also constituted a system of meaning and as such had a sacred character.

By choosing the nation as the effective intermediate group in which and through which social solidarity in the modern world was to be realized, Durkheim took a problematic decision, for how was he going to avoid the possible excesses of nationalism? His solution was simple: the nation had always to be conscious of the fact that it formed part of the wider world and its values had therefore to be in accordance with the universal values of mankind. State absolutism had to be checked by the counterbalancing action of secondary groups. Still, one is left with a feeling of uneasiness, for the very idea that the nation is to be viewed as a sacred entity and as a provider of existential meaning seems to produce a kind of particularism, which is out of tune with these wider ideals. In the essay on Durkheim, it is maintained that this created a profound ambiguity, which permeated much of what he wrote on morality and religion. Maybe, Durkheim should never have accepted the role of national moral scientist, but it is equally arguable that this would have deprived us of some of the most penetrating insights that we have gained through his interest in the religious character of social life.

The second essay in this volume questions Weber's view that formal rationality, which he saw as the key characteristic of modern capitalism, is to be regarded as more or less the exclusive product of the puritanical tradition. The question is not new, as it has cropped up time and again over the past sixty years. Readers will be familair with Tawney's argument that the first stirrings of modern capitalism manifested themselves already in the Catholic Middle Ages, and they will be equally familiar with the view that it was the minority status of the Puritans rather than their theological orientation, which led to the development of capitalism in their midst. The argument developed in the present essay is different and in a sense also more radical, as it posits that formal rationality is not only to be seen in relation to the content but also the form of an ethical system. More specifically, it is argued that a distinction has to be made between single and plural systems, and that single systems have a much more pronounced tendency towards that type of rationality. The puritanical tradition was such a single system, but it was not the only one, nor can it be maintained that single ethical systems are a typical product of the West. It is further suggested that single ethical systems tend to combine with a marked degree of rationality in the economic systems with which they are connected. This vieuw, then, throws a different light on the Weber thesis, as it introduces a variable which hitherto has not been taken into account.

National consciousness and economic development are the two main issues in the new nations. Everywhere, countries formed by the vagaries of colonialism are in search of a national identity, and everywhere they are trying to set up a viable economy. These two issues are by no means unconnected, for the incessant drive to develop the economy is invariably linked with nationalist symbols and sentiments. People are told to modernize their methods of production, to work harder and produce more, for the sake of the country. Durkheim's view of the nation as a sacred entity is verified time and again, wherever new countries mobilize their citizens for major economic efforts. Ethical systems, once different from tribe to tribe, are replaced by single systems, allowing the new nations to rationalize their economies and come to terms with the modern world. This should be sufficient to prove the continued relevance of the themes broached in this volume, but it would be a mistake to think that nation worship is something confined to the Third World. The experience of the Third Reich has taught us otherwise.

M.S.
D.M.

Table of Contents

Ch. I Clan religion and civil religion
    Introduction 13
1 Civil religion in America 17
2 Theocracies, reconciliation systems and political religion 23
3 Durkheim's theory of religion 28
  3.1 The clan and its religion 30
  3.2 The individual and the clan 34
  3.3 Real or ideal society? 36
  3.4 Durkheim's conception of civil religion 36
4 Turner's structure and communitas 43
  4.1 Durkheim and Turner 46
5 Concluding remarks 49
    Bibliography 51

Ch. II Singular and plural ethical systems
    Introduction 54
1 The Weber thesis 55
  1.1 The Protestant ethic 55
  1.2 Capitalism and modern capitalism 57
2 Judaism and capitalism 60
  2.1 Judaism: traditional or modern capitalism? 60
  2.2 Judaism: the debate between Weber and Sombart 66
3 Capitalism and ethic in India and China 74
  3.1 Hinduism 74
  3.2 Buddhism 76
  3.3 Jainism 78
  3.4 Religion in China 80
4 Conclusion 84
    Notes 89
    Bibliography 92

Clan religion and civil religion: on Durkheim's conception of God as a symbol of society

by Matthew Schoffeleers

Introduction

This essay has been written with the sole purpose of examining the logic and the implications of Durkheim's theory of religion as it applies to the modern state. It was prompted in the first place by R. N. Bellah's well-known article on civil religion in America, which is very much in the Durkheimian tradition and which clearly manifests the weaknesses of that tradition (Bellah 1970). What I object to in Bellah's article is its implicit identification of the state with the nation and its explicit identification of American civil religion with the religious self-definition of the American people as a whole. I am not the first person to criticize Bellah; others have done so before me, some of them even going to the extreme of accusing him of state idolization. This is simply unwarranted as the whole tenor of his article testifies against such an interpretation. In order to bring out the differences between Bellah's picture of civil religion and what these critics refer to we shall in this essay make use of David Apter's distinction between the religious reflexes of what he calls reconciliation systems and mobilization systems (Apter 1963). By the former he means a state organisation in which various conflicting interests are brought together under a corpus of common law, which has itself religious or quasi-religious significance, as it stands ultimately above the different interest groups. Mobilization systems on the other hand, are characterized by the total or near-total politicisation of public life, the suppression of dissent, the prevalence of the person of the leader over common law, and the pronounced sacralization of political doctrine. These, of course, are ideal types which unsually tend to hybridize.
It is generally agreed that one of the foci of Durkheim's theory of religion is its integrative potential in respect of human collectivities, typified in primitive religions by the clan, and in modern secular religions by the nation. From either viewpoint - clan or nation - the integration thesis raises questions with regard to the occurrence of

internal as well as external oppression. Durkheim, as we shall have occasion to show, was clearly concerned with this problem, at least as it manifests itself in the modern world, but he has little to say about its relevance to primitive communities, on the one hand because the ethnography at his disposal did not contain much significant information on this issue, and on the other hand because he appeared to be somewhat wedded to Rousseau's idea of the noble savage. At any rate, he seems to have been so captivated by their rituals of solidarity, that it eclipsed the opposite view of primitive man's life as being nasty, brutish and short. With regard to the modern situation, however, Durkheim was quite outspoken. He repeatedly warns against the ever-present danger of internal and external oppression which, he argues, can only be avoided if state organisations explicitly subscribe to a philosophy of moral individualism, and if they allow secondary groups to act as a counter-balancing mechanism (Bellah 1973a: xxxiii-xxxvi).

Yet there is a curious ambivalence in all of Durkheim's writings on religion, which appears for instance where he discusses the transition from the religion of the clan to the religion of the tribe (Durkheim 1915: 283-294). In that context he argues that the two may be contrasted in terms of totem worship and the worship of supernatural beings such as gods. Totem worship may be described as a kind of religion which heavily emphasizes the values and interests of a particular community, whereas the worship of supernatural beings implies their subordination to a set of wider ideals and values. The contrast is thus one between particularism and universalism. One would expect Durkheim to comment on the obvious tensions which their co-existence must of necessity provoke. That hope is not fulfilled though, for in Durkheim's descriptions of primitive societies there is no room for conflict. Thus the values of the smaller units, the clans, are seen as being in harmony with those of the larger units of which they form part. The same could not be said, however, of modern society in which tensions between national and wider values were very much in evidence. Durkheim recognized this, and he was quite outspoken in his condemnation of every form of narrow nationalism, which he rejected as immoral and as a return to paganism (Wallace 1977: 288). Even so, he propounded a conception of the nation and the state, which came dangerously close to the very thing he condemned. The ideal nation in this conception was the equivalent of a congregation of believers, and one of the jobs of the state was to watch over its orthodoxy (Bellah 1973a: xxxv). In other words, by explicitly according nation and state a sacred character he could be interpreted, and has repeatedly been interpreted, as advocating a nationalist mentality. True, part of the orthodoxy was that universal values had to prevail over national values, but that was more easily said than done, for the very elevation of the nation to the status of the sacred would act as a major obstacle to a balanced judgement.

At this point we may introduce three observations which are fundamental to the argument developed in this paper. In the first place, the suggestion that state-based religious or quasi-religious doctrines - whether they emerge from historical experience, as in Bellah's case, or from a combination of historical factors and systematic theorizing, as in Durkheim's case - are always particularistic, as they rest on the assumption that the state is homologous whith the nation, and that the nation in its turn is to be seen as a homogeneous body. Such doctrines generally deny the existence of disagreement within the collectivity, and, by sacralizing that same collectivity, they tend to present it as a kind of superior being.

The second observation is that internal dissent may also express itself by means of religion, the point being that a civil religion, where it exists and to the extent that it exists, may be challenged by counter-religions, which are as much part of the national life as is the official religion.

Finally, it is suggested that not only do religious systems conflict with each other - and thereby modify each other -, but that each individual system also carries within its own universe the seeds of its negation. One of the most imaginative contributions in this field has been made by the anthropologist V. W. Turner. In his book, *The Ritual Process* (Turner 1974), he argues on the basis of a wealth of empirical evidence that religion may sacralize both 'structure' - by which he means broadly the existing organisational arrangements of a collectivity - and 'anti-structure' or 'communitas'. Structure and communitas are two major models of human relations, one of which articulates and legitimates differentation and inequality, while the other emphasizes 'humankindness', the view that all men are ultimately equal. If social life is to be viable, it must combine these two elements, for structure without the tempering influence of communitas would soon become arid and oppressive.

It will not be difficult to see that Turner's theory is directly relevant to our discussion of Bellah and Durkheim, for the problem in both cases is that they seem to sacralize the state structure at the expense of human freedom. I deliberately use the word 'seem', since neither of these two authors had any intention of advocating state worship. Speaking in human terms, they had in a sense too much confidence in the institutions of the modern democratic state. Speaking in terms of social theory, they seemed somehow unwilling to account for the manifold tensions and conflicts within and between national collectivities. Their accounts of civil religion therefore leave us with a feeling of unreality, the roots of which we are trying to expose.

Civil religion in America

Bellah begins his article by establishing in what ways his view of a national religion differs from that of other commentators, who either saw Christianity as the national faith or who saw the various churches as collectively engaged in a generalized religion of 'The American Way of Life'. His own reading of the situation is that "there actually exists alongside of and rather clearly differentiated from the churches an elaborate and well-institutionalized civil religion in America". This religion, or religious dimension, "has its own seriousness and integrity and requires the same care in understanding that any other religion does" (Bellah 1970: 168). But how and where does this civil religion manifest itself? Bellah points out that the inaugural addresses of the various Presidents contain credal formulas which appear crucial to the subject under consideration. One of these is the expression of belief in a transcendent God to whom not only the President but all citizens are ultimately responsible. The word 'God' in this context appears to symbolize the rights of men which are more basic than any political structure, and which provide a point of revolutionary leverage from which the state structure may be radically altered. But, apart from making any form of political absolutism illegitimate, it also provides a transcendent goal for the political process: It is not to be an end in itself but the fulfilment of God's will on earth. This, it is maintained, was the motivating spirit of those who founded America, and it has been present in every generation since (Bellah o.c.: 172).

One of the most impressive parts of Bellah's paper is that in which he traces the history of the nation's religious self-definition and, closely related to this, the development of what may be called a history of salvation.

"Until the Civil War, the American civil religion focused above all on the event of the Revolution, which was seen as the final act of the Exodus from the old lands across the waters. The Declaration of Independence and the Constitution were the sacred scriptures and Washington the divinely appointed Moses who led his people out of the hands of tyranny. The Civil War (...) was the second great event that involved the national self-understanding so deeply as to require expression in the civil religion" (Bellah o.c.: 176).

That event raised the deepest questions of national meaning, both in respect of America's internal relations, in which slavery stood out as the central focus of a generalized feeling of guilt, and in respect of America's meaning for the whole world. The themes of death, sacrifice and rebirth, as symbolized in the life and death of Lincoln, emerged out of that experience. If the earlier symbolism of the civil religion had been Hebraic, without in any specific sense being Jewish, the post-bellum symbolism was Christian without having specific links with the Christian Church (Bellah o.c.: 178). If the earlier symbolism found its ritual expression in the institution of Thanksgiving Day, which served to integrate the family into the civil religion, the new symbolism expressed itself in Memorial Day which integrated the local community into the national cult. Along with the four other holidays, including the birthdays of Washington and Lincoln, they constitute the annual ritual calendar of the civil religion of America.

In the next part of his paper Bellah discusses the relations between the churches and civil religion as well as some of the less positive aspects of the national religion. Although the churches have at times criticized what appeared to them to be superficial or idolizing aspects of its tenets, there have never been any deep-rooted conflicts as was the case for instance in France, where a virulent anti-clericalism led to attempts to set up an anti-Christian civil religion. As for its negative aspects, Bellah points to the tendency on the domestic scene, at times to fuse God, country and flag to attack non-conformist and liberal ideas and groups of all kinds. Still, such tendencies are said to develop outside the tradition of civil religion rather than within it, as the John Birch Society demonstrates, when it attacks the central American symbol of Democracy itself. The danger of distortion, however, is greater, with respect to the field of international politics where such utterly shameful enterprises as the Vietnam war have been justified with reference to America's role as the New Jerusalem. The reason for this, as Bellah sees it, is that in the field of external relations the built-in safeguards of the tradition are weaker, because the majority of the people are unable to judge the facts for what they are (Bellah o.c.: 182).

What of the future of civil religion? Like much of church religion, it is at present in the throes of a theological crisis, which questions its very belief in the supernatural and which may possibly result in the progressive inability of the central symbol to act as a unifying factor. This is related to what Bellah calls "America's third time of trial", which he defines as the problem of taking responsible action in a revolutionary world. More specifically, this entails the replacement of a manichean view of world politics as a confrontation between East and West with a vision that sees the whole of mankind engaged in a struggle against tyranny, poverty, disease and war, wherever these may occur. If this third time of trial will be negotiated successfully, - that is, if America will be able to help attain a viable and coherent world order - this would precipitate a major new set of symbolic forms. American civil religion would then become part of a new civil religion of the world, which would be a fulfilment and not a denial of the present national religion, for such an outcome has been its eschatological hope from the beginning (Bellah o.c.: 186). American civil religion is, so Bellah concludes, a heritage of moral and religious experience from which the nation still has much to learn, as it formulates the decisions that lie ahead.

So much for this 'by now famous article' as Parsons rightly calls it (Parsons 1973: 164). I have tried to do it as much justice as possible in the relatively short space available, but the omission of the rich documentation collated by Bellah to illustrate his argument must of necessity weaken the power of my presentation. To the extent that such is the case, readers are advised to turn to the original paper.

The value of Bellah's article derives from the fact that it is an attempt to identify the religious self-conception of a vast, highly modernized, and in many ways very diversified society. In addition to this, it may also be regarded as an attempt to answer a perplexing question left over by Durkheim, who had posited that every viable society has a religious view of itself, which makes it into a moral community or a church. Such a thing is perhaps not too difficult to accept with regard to theocracies or tribal communities, but, as Parsons remarks, "in modern societies, with the differentiation and later the separation of church and state, it is by by no means a simple and obvious question in what sense what is usually called a secular society, if it is to be a society at all, should also be called a church" (Parsons o.c.: 164). In Parsons' opinion, Bellah has shown that precisely in the Durkheimian sense, the American societal community does indeed have a religion, with a relatively full panoply of beliefs and practices, and that this can be considered both constitutive of and expressing the moral community which constitutes the nation. Bellah has thus done what Durkheim omitted to do, as the latter occupied himself with a blue-print for modern civil religion rather than the empirical study of civil religion as it actually operates. The results of Bellah's analysis is that, in a sense, we can now view Durkheim's idea put to practice.

After the publication of Bellah's article, it came under a good deal of criticism, the major objection being that the religious system described by him was little more than a form of national selfworship (Bellah 1970: 168). Bellah's defence against this was that his critics had misread him, as the civil religious tradition contained within itself precisely those critical principles which undercut the ever-present danger of self-idolization. The discussion really turned around two different but related problems: Is Bellah's description of America civil religion 'factually correct', and if so, what are we to think of that religion in terms of its normative content? Bellah answers the first of these questions with a quote from Wallace Stevens to the effect that we live in the description of a place and not in the place itself. In other words, social reality is what people think it is and to the extent that those involved recognize themselves in Bellah's picture, that picture is to be considered factually correct. The very fact that Bellah's notion gained wide currency, wider by comparison than similar notions in the field, seems therefore to testify to its validity (Bellah 1973b: 9).

My own reaction after reading it was: And what of the Americans of African and Indian descent? Would they subscribe to this theology, this history of salvation, which has apparently been formulated by Americans of European origin? For what is seen by the latter as a journey to the promised land was to the former the way to a profoundly degrading life of slavery. There is little reason to doubt either the sincerity of Bellah or the potential for sincerity in the religion he describes, but it is an illusion to think that it represents the religious self-definition of the nation as distinct from the state. Much as one hates to say this, it is ultimately a construct which has originated and developed among those that were closest to the seats of power and those that felt they could identify with them. This is not so much a charge against American civil religion and its influential theologian as an invitation to rethink the issue and to look for communal religious reflexes which are different from and in varying degrees antagonistic to, the concepts and values of the civil religion. It would not be possible, one should think, to write an equally compelling account of, say, the religious self-definition of the black population and the way it conceives of its own history of salvation. Such an account no doubt would provide us with a quite different interpretation of the same set of events. The conclusion I would like to draw for the moment is that a civil religion is apparently not the same as a national religion, at least not in a modern democratic state. Where the two are congruent, one finds Apter's political religion (Apter 1963). At the national level civil religion needs to be challenged by counter-religions, be these represented by the churches, the John Birch Society, the Black Muslims or whatever other groups, if it is to retain whatever openness or sense of the transcendent it possesses. A civil religion does not necessarily have this openness because it professes a belief in a transcendental God. Its belief in a God who scrutinizes human action is to a vital extent dependent on the action of antagonistic groups.

In a follow-up article which carried the title "American Civil Religion in the 1970's", Bellah shows himself considerably more receptive to the dialectical process by which religious self-definition is constantly created and recreated (Bellah 1973b). Referring to Nixon's second inaugural address in which the old myth of American innocence was blatantly resurrected, he comes to the conclusion not only that civil religion may be subject to misuse - as he had maintained in his earlier article - but also that it contains within itself various and conflicting strands. He also sees it as being challenged on a massive scale by the young, by students, by ethnic groups and by the women's movement (Bellah o.c.: 15). Consequently, he urges a profound re-examination of the civil religious tradition by subjecting everything to the most searing criticism; something that goes far beyond simply distinguishing the good tradition from the bad tradition, but *a criticism that sees the seeds of the bad in the good and vice-versa*. Bellah also sees the necessity of relativizing the American civil religious tradition by viewing it as part of the wider movement toward human liberation which is taking place in our days (Bellah o.c.: 16; italics mine).

But what, we may ask, will remain of American civil religion when all these operations have been completed, suppose such a thing would be possible? In all likelihood nothing, despite Bellah's good intentions, for every single concept, value or myth would be found wanting. The conclusion of it all is that Bellah, who in quite a real sense brought American civil religion into being, has at the same time become one of the agents of its destruction. The point which he misses in his second article is that he places himself squarely outside the fold of civil religion, since he redefines it in a way which makes it unrecognizable to its believers. In the next section we shall explore the possible causes of Bellah's equivocal position.

Theocracies, reconciliation systems and political religion 2.

David Apter, in a well-known study of the religious reflexes of the state, has suggested that these may be subsumed under three categories, which may be called theocratic religion, church religion and political religion (Apter 1963). His particular concern in the study we are referring to is with Third World countries, but much of what he has to say is universally applicable, and we may therefore use it to apply a comparative framework for the present discussion.

Apter gives us two definitions of religion; one from the viewpoint of the collectivity, the other from the viewpoint of the individuals making up that collectivity. From the former viewpoint then, religion is defined as that which is concerned with the sacred, *i.e.* ideas and objects that, socially understood, are exceptionally venerated (Apter o.c.: 87). The sacred is thus, functionally speaking, a stabilizing element, for it marks off what is considered inviolable in a society. Religion, however, is also a set of transcendental beliefs which meet certain fundamental needs of individuals, notably the need of giving meaning to death, the need of establishing an individual personality and the need of identifying objectives in life (Apter o.c.: 89). These definitions are, as we shall see, fully within the Durkheimian tradition, and they are at the same time sufficiently close to Bellah's conception to ensure an overall unity of discourse. What concerns us here is the degree to which state organisations are experienced as manifestations of the sacred, and the degree to which state organisations meet or aim at meeting the fundamental needs of individuals as defined by Apter. There is of course a connection between these two elements, for a state organisation, if it is to meet those needs, has to possess sacred qualities.

Apter's categorization, moreover, has a distinct developmental aspect insofar as it accounts also for the genetic links between different modes of sacralization. Thus, political religion is seen as having emerged, historically speaking, after and in a sense also out of church religion, which in its turn is viewed as having evolved from the theocratic mode. In the present stage of human history, they represent the three global options open to state organisations. We shall first describe the general characteristics of each and then see what light they throw on Bellah's dilemma.

In theocracies, political and religious associations are one and the same. Some specialisation of political roles is possible, but these have their significance in a religious system. The king is a spiritual counselor as well as a warrior; he is a defender of the faith in addition to being a lawgiver. Many forms of leadership are possible, but leaders have two major qualities. First, they are roles that are personalized and institutionalized. Second, they are respresentatives of the deity. Their autonomy derives from them, even if they are elected by the public at large (Apter o.c.: 72). Theocracies are communities that are part of a natural and wider order both of nature and transcendence. There is thus no sharp distinction between the natural universe and the state, nor is there a sharp dividing line between the living and the dead, nor the real state and the transcendent state, that is, between the kingdom of man and the kingdom of God. Laws tend to be linked to custom, ritual and other religious practices (Apter o.c.: 72).

Theocratic societies, though generally sharing these qualities, are nevertheless of a great variety, for under this category virtually all primitive political communities and most societies of the ancient world can be subsumed, including those of Greece and Rome, as well as some of the modern Islamic states. While referring to classic Greece as a theocracy, Apter quotes some passages from the political historian E. Barker which are so reminiscent of Durkheim's blueprint for civil religion that we cannot leave them unmentioned. In the Greek polis, it is said:

> "...the state exists for the moral development and perfection of its individual members. It is the fulfilment and perfection of the individual which means - and it is the only thing which means - the perfection of the state. A state which is meant for the moral perfection of its members will be an educational institution. Its laws will serve to make men good. Thus its offices ideally will belong to men of virtue who have moral discernment. Its chief activity will be that of training and sustaining the mature in the way of righteousness. That is why

we may speak of such a state as really a church: like Calvin's church it exercises a 'holy discipline'. Political philosophy thus becomes a sort of moral theology" (Apter o.c.: 70).

Mutatis mutandis, one may see the same elements also in Durkheim's description of Australian aboriginal communities, in which the individual derives his personal identity as well as his moral objectives and his general philosophy of life from the political community through the initiation ceremony and a plethora of other rituals. Generally speaking, then, religion as conceived in terms of the communally sacred and as conceived in terms of the existential needs of the individual appear to be largely identical within the theocratic mode.

Church religion occurs in what Apter calls a 'reconciliation system', which is most aptly expressed in the phrase 'a government of laws and not of men'. By this is meant not only the requirement that men obey laws, a characteristic of all viable communities, but rather that law has a wider wisdom than that of any individual man. As such, its status is venerated for its own sake (Apter o.c.: 73). This preoccupation with law, however, was not the only factor relevant to the development of a reconciliation system. The second was the separation of church and state, of temporal and spiritual jurisdictions (Apter o.c.: 74). The significance of this was that it provided a philosophical legitimation for limiting the power of the executive, for
"...the concept of checks and balances implies a faith that such a system helps to restore the governance of men to a natural harmony in which the individual's true nature is one of freedom within civil society. Civil society ruled by law is in turn reinforced by spiritual sanction on an individual basis. Indeed, Protestantism helped to reinforce this doctrine so that right conduct, guided by Christian ethic, and individual freedom, tempered by representative government, were mutually reinforcing elements. The result was a high degree of self-restraint being the essence of the liberal democratic polity" (Apter o.c.: 76).

Politics under such a system of necessity takes on a pluralistic and contingent character. There exist diverse centres of power which must be reconciled when basic decisions are made (Apter o.c.: 64). Even the value system is relativistic to a significant degree, for all values can change except two. One is the dignity of the individual, which can only be preserved through the dignity of law. The second is the principle of representative government (Apter o.c.: 76). From the viewpoint of the present discussion, the important thing to note is that, under a reconciliation system, individuals no longer need derive their personality and meaning systems from a state-centred religious system. What they demand of the state is rather the protection of individual rights and values insofar as these are not considered antagonistic to the common good. Still, although the separation between church and state has been a fact of life for several centuries, the church, while its authority remained intact, was able to share the state's responsibility for the running of social life (Apter o.c.: 67). The decline of religion, however, has imposed on the western democratic polity the singular problem of how to provide alternative sources of meaning, faith, and spiritual sustenance that all men need to some degree. Our present crisis is one of unsatisfied moral ambitions, and our political framework mirrors faithfully this weakness (Apter o.c.: 77).

The third reflex of the state structure considered by Apter is political religion. Its defining characteristic is that the state once again acts as the provider of individual meaning and purpose. It does this no longer indirectly through the mediation of a belief in trancendental beings as in the theocratic system, but directly in the person of its leader becoming the object of worship and devotion. Political religion arose in the west as a response to the loss of faith that characterizes present reconciliation systems. By no longer placing reliance on church religion, one of the stabilizing elements that originally supported the political framework in reconciliation systems, the sacred, is employed in many new nations - and has recently been employed by the fascist, nazi and some of the marxist regimes - to develop a system of political legitimacy and to aid in mobilizing the community for secular ends. Once political doctrine has been made into political belief, efforts are made to formalize that faith as a means by which to achieve major aims (Apter o.c.: 77). Such a system is characterized by Apter as a 'mobilization system' which rests on an implicit assumption:

> "That which divides men from one another is due to unnatural causes - colonialism, neocolonialism, classes which derive their differences from hostile relationships centring around property. Men must be freed from these unnatural differences by both acts of leadership and exceptional public will. Harmony in the political sphere derives from the messianic leader who points out the dangers and noxious poisons of faction. Many such

leaders are charismatic who represent the 'one'. They personify the monistic quality of the system" (Apter o.c.: 78).

What loses out of course is the idea of individualism. The peculiar genius of our civilisation, that is, the relationship between individualism and law, is viewed as imprisoning, reactionary and parochial (Apter o.c.: 77). What is required is the individual's total belief in and support of the cause.

If we are to apply these three modes to Bellah's picture of American civil religion we may perhaps say that he described what amounts to a theocratic religion, which he himself interpreted as a reconciliation religion, while his critics preferred to view it as a mobilization religion. The theocratic element is evident in the conception of America as one nation, a chosen people, a country under the proven guidance of God. The suggestion of a political religion is evoked by the fact that Bellah's account has a distinct, though unintended, mobilizing ring, at least to non-Americans and to the disaffected within America. One reason for this differential perception is that political religion is by its very nature so close to theocratic religion. The real obverse of the theocratic system is not the mobilization type but the reconciliation type. In both the theocratic and the mobilization type, the individual derives - or is supposed to derive - his personality and meaning system from the state, be it in a different sense in each case. What differentiates the reconciliation type from both of these is precisely the negation of this requirement. It cannot have a communal symbol of meaning except a symbol which affirms the legitimacy of individualism and hence of diversity. To the extent that a communal symbol requires adhesion to a value other than that of individualism, a society moves either in the direction of a theocracy or a political religion. This is precisely what seems to be the case in the civil religion of America, for it affirms that politics is not an end in itself but the fulfilment of God's will on earth. If there is one thing typical of the theocratic mode, it is this. Within a reconciliation system a government cannot hold such a belief without alienating itself in principle from its primary objective, for by the fact of associating itself with a religious universe, and by defining its goals and actions in terms of that universe, its steps outside its sphere of competence. If it is to be honest to God, it has to dissociate itself from God. The searing criticism, which Bellah urges should be applied to civil religion, can logically come to no other conclusion.

Durkheim's theory of religion 3.

One striking difference between Bellah's and Durkheim's accounts of civil religion is that in Bellah's case the nation still adheres to belief in a transcendental God, while in Durkheim's case that belief is entirely absent. The reason for this is of course that wide-spread secularization of public life did come much earlier to Europe than to America. Particularly in France, where the educational system had come to be fully laicized under the Third Republic, this created a problem of the first order, which was that of providing moral education. One of those who came to be actively involved in that problem was Durkheim, and it was in that context that he developed his sociology of religion.

It is, I think, correct to say that Durkheim's major interest, as far as religion was concerned, moved between primitive Australian and modern civil religion. The first of these interests found its clearest and most comprehensive expression in *The Elementary Forms of the Religious Life,* which was published in 1912 (Eng. trans. Durkheim 1915). The second is particularly evident in *Moral Education,* which was composed in the years before 1912 and published posthumously in 1925 (Eng. trans. Durkheim 1973).

Modern morality, in Durkheim's conception, was to be based on empirically verifiable principles and not on some religious creed, for religion in the traditional sense of belief in a supernatural reality had become unacceptable. Another requirement would be that it was to enunciate truths that were universally valid and capable of expressing and promoting positive relationships between nations (Bellah 1973a: xv, xvii-xviii). During the earlier part of his career, till about 1895, Durkheim did not seem to have perceived any intrinsic relationship between morality and religion. In his later period, however, he came to think of religion as the element which gives public morality the unquestioned authority it must have, if it is to function properly. The meaning of this change can only be understood against the background of the evolution of Durkheim's thinking on religion, which, broadly speaking, had moved from the position that religion is to be regarded as a social phenomenon to the position that society itself was a religious phenomenon. The later position, however, is not to be viewed as a negation of the earlier one; it rather deepens and complements it. In his earlier phase he tended to see religion as an attribute of society, something essential or at least useful to its proper functioning. In his later phase, religion became the very source of social life, for it was through religion that society generated and continuously regenerated itself. Consequently, every viable society, insofar as it was viable, had to have a religious conception of itself. This was quite a novel idea; an idea, moreover, which possessed a distinct heuristic potential, for it could instigate the kind of enquiry that Bellah undertook in relation to the United States of America.

It is always difficult to trace the roots of a seminal concept, and so it is in this case. Durkheim himself refers to his reading of Robertson Smith's *The Religion of the Semites* as a decisive factor (Lukes 1975: 237). It may be, as others have pointed out, that the almost religious enthusiasm generated by the Dreyfuss Affair among a large section of the French intellectuals of that time, contributed to it. On the other hand, it may be argued that neither event would have had the meaning it actually had for Durkheim, if he had not already moved a long way in that direction. The roots go therefore much deeper, and their ultimate feeding ground has to be sought in Durkheim's passionate patriotism. It was this that gave direction to much of what he did and wrote. It was his hope that one day France would be able to overcome the virulent factionalism which had kept her divided for so long, and that she once again would be able to experience the feeling of national solidarity.

It was the Australian clan and its religion, which in quite a vital sense stood model for what nationhood could be and could do for modern man, and it is therefore no coincidence that certain parts of his description of Australian clan religion find their distinct echo in his writings on national moral education. Still, by emphasizing the nation and nationhood as agents for the promotion of social solidarity in the modern world, he took a step which landed him in the midst of contradiction and ambiguity, which were only aggravated by his conception of the nation as a religious or quasi-religious entity. It is not that Durkheim engaged in theoretical fantasies. As we have seen, his theory of religion is very much applicable to theocracies and mobilization systems. The contradictions to which we are referring are more directly apparent in reconciliation systems, and it was with these that Durkheim was ultimately concerned. However, we shall also argue that, even in his analysis of a primitive theocratic system, Durkheim ran into problems which he could not, or at any rate did not, solve.

3.1 *The clan and its religion*

The principal notions in Durkheim's account of Australian aboriginal religion are totem and clan, for these two imply each other. A clan organisation can only have totemism for its religious reflex, while totemism in its turn is always linked up with a clan organisation. If a social organisation based on clans is the simplest we know, the same can be said of totemism in regard of religion (Durkheim 1915: 167, 187).

The clan consists of a group of kindred who are not, or not necessarily, related by ties of consanguinity but by a common name, which is that of a natural phenomenon, usually a species belonging to the animal or vegetal world. These natural phenomena, called totems, are not only proper to clans. There are also totems that belong to phratries and marriage classes. Finally, the Australians also have individual totems, which act as guardians of persons, and sexual totems (Durkheim o.c.: 107-113, 157-166). There are no two clans that have the same name and the same totem. Clan names, and therefore clan totems, are inherited through the father's or the mother's line, depending on the organisation of the tribe, but sometimes they are acquired in a more or less fortuitous manner (Durkheim o.c.: 107).

The totem is not only a name but also an emblem. Abstract representations of it are painted on a person's apparel and body, or engraved on various objects. Since such representations are only made and used in a ritual context, it appears that they have a sacred character. This is particularly the case with the so-called *churingas,* which are oblong pieces of wood or polished stone upon which the totemic emblem is engraved. These objects are kept secluded in special places, and they are not be seen or touched by the non-initiated. Even the places where they are kept are sacred, for they serve as sanctuaries to those in danger of their lives. Not only the emblems are sacred but also - be it to a lesser degree - the vegetal or animal species which they represent, as well as the individuals belonging to the totemic community. The sacredness of totemic animals and plants is expressed by the various interdictions with which they are surrounded. Man's sacredness derives from the fact that he bears the name of the totem and, by the same token, regards himself as to a certain extent identical with it (Durkheim o.c.: 113-140).

Next, Durkheim shows how the entire universe is integrated in the totemic system. Astral bodies, plants, animals and features of the landscape, all are categorized in terms of phratries and clans, and all are to a greater or lesser extent considered sacred. Totemism, apart from being the religious reflex of the clan organisation, is therefore also to be seen as an authentic cosmology (Durkheim o.c.: 141-166).

Having come to this point, Durkheim makes his first major statement on the relations between clans as religious units. Although each totem is only venerated in its corresponding clan, they nevertheless form a single system within the same tribe:

"...in order to from an adequate idea of totemism, we must not confine ourselves within the limits of the clan, but must consider the tribe as a whole. It is true that the particular cult of each clan enjoys a very great autonomy; we can now see that it is within the clan that the active ferment of the religious life takes place. But it is also true that these cults fit into each other, and the totemic religion is a complex system formed by their union, just as Greek polytheism was made by the union of all particular cults addressed to the different divinities (Durkheim o.c.: 156)."

The reader is thus given the impression that totemic religion resembles Greek polytheism, in which the gods form a pantheon, and in which the faithful may address themselves to one or the other god according to their needs. Nothing could be farther from the truth, for it appears that

"The cult celebrated there (*i.e.* in the totemic clan; M.S.), though not a self-sufficing whole, has only external relations with the others; they interchange without intermingling; the totem of the clan is only sacred to this clan" (Durkheim o.c.: 196)."

The same principle extends to the totemic cosmology, for

"...the group of things attributed to each clan, which are part of it the same way the men are, have the same individuality and autonomy. Each of them is represented as irreducible into similar groups, as separated from them by a break of continuity, and as constituting a distinct realm" (Durkheim *ibid*)".

It appears, therefore, that we have to view totemism at the tribal level as consisting of a number of religions, which are all of the same morphological type, but which are otherwise independent. What is sacred to one clan is not sacred to another. Nor is this all, for the abyss between these religions is so great that their adherents cannot perceive of them as different manifestations of the same thing:
> "Under these circumstances it would occur to noone that these heterogeneous worlds were different manifestations of one and the same fundamental force; *on the contrary, one might suppose that each of them corresponded to an organically different mana* (i.e. fundamental religious force; M.S.) whose action could not extend beyond the clan and the circle of things attributed to it" (Durkheim, *ibid;* my italics).

Australian totemism is thus something very different from, say, African ancestor veneration, in which members of individual lineages, although paying their respects to different supernatural beings, believe these to be of one kind. They see them as different manifestations of the same thing. Apparently, this is not so in Australian totemism, for
> "The idea of a single and universal mana could only be born at the moment when the tribal religion developed above that of the clans and *absorbed them more of less completely*. It is along with the feeling of tribal unity that the feeling of the substantial unity of the world awakens" (Durkheim *ibid;* my italics).

Here, Durkheim begins to develop the idea that Australian religion manifests itself in two forms: as a reflex of the clan, and as a reflex of the tribe. Clan religion is inherently particularistic, as it is incapable of transcending itself; tribal religion, on the other hand, may be seen as the beginning of a universalistic orientation. Durkheim goes on to state that religion at the tribal and intertribal level is characterized by belief in gods, who are to be considered as the equivalents of national and international religious symbols (Durkheim 1915: 273-296, 415). There is no discontinuity, though, for the notion of spirits and gods has historically developed from the totemic principle:
> "In fact, the tribal God is only an ancestral spirit who finally won a pre-eminent place. The ancestral spirits are only entities

forged in the image of the individual souls whose origin they are destined to explain. The souls in their turn, are only the form taken by the impersonal forces which we found at the basis of totemism, as they individualize themselves in the human body. The unity of the system is as great as its complexity" (Durkheim o.c.: 295).

Gods are the representatives of the universalist element in Australian religion, and it is therefore an error to think that only the great religions possess this characteristic:
"From the dawn of history, religious beliefs have manifested a tendency to overflow out of one strictly limited political society; it is as though they had a natural aptitude for crossing frontiers, and for diffusing and internationalizing themselves. Of course there have been peoples and times when this spontaneous aptitude has been held in check by opposed social necessities; but that does not keep it from being real and, as we see, very primitive" (Durkheim o.c.: 289).

Durkheim remains inconclusive as to the way these two types of religion relate to each other. In one of the texts quoted above he suggests that religion at the tribal level can only develop to the extent that the clan structure is absorbed, while on other occasions he conveys the impression that they can co-exist and in fact do co-exist. Totemic religion, or the particularistic type, appears at the base of the social structure, by which he means the clan organization. Worship of gods, or the universalistic type of religion, appears at the top, by which Durkheim means the tribal and intertribal organisation (Durkheim o.c.: 425). If there are tensions between the two types, he does not mention them.

There is one other feature to which we may draw attention, which is that Durkheim in his description of Australian religion pays much more attention to the clan than to the tribe. The clan is the unit within which "the active ferment of the religious life takes place" (Durkheim o.c.: 156), and it is within the context of clan religion that he develops his notion of divinity as the symbol and transfiguration of society (Durkheim o.c.: 205-214). Finally, it is from clan religion that tribal religion evolves. Clan religion contains all elements of the more develop religions except one: universalism. To obtain that one element, Durkheim has to make his clans into a tribe, but he can make them into a tribe only insofar as they cease to be clans. That, in a nutshell, was his problem. One can follow Durkheim's struggle with this problem throughout his book, but he never seems to come to a satisfactory conclusion, because it was the old problem of nationalism versus universalism in a different guise.

3.2 *The individual and the clan*
From the earlier stages of his career Durkheim had maintained that respect for the dignity and the rights of the individual were in the process of becoming the central dogma of an emerging universal religion. This new religion was thus to be the opposite of primitive religion, which he continued to see as primarily group-oriented. Still, since he also held that totemic religion contained in germinal form all essential elements of the more developed religions, one of his tasks was to be the identification of the individualistic traits in totemism. Durkheim thought he could discern these in the so-called individual cults, which included the worship of personal totems and ancestral guardians.

It appeared that in the Australian communities every individual was allowed to choose for himself a totem whose name would be his own first name. Between a person and his totem - usually an animal - there existed the closest possible bonds, for it was thought that he participated in the nature of that animal to the point of being able, in certain circumstances, to change into its form. On its part, the animal acted as his guide and guardian (Durkheim o.c.: 157-159). Ancestral spirits fulfilled more or less the same role. They, too, were the object of private worship and, like the totemic animals, they were believed to help and protect their devotee (Durkheim o.c.: 279). The difference between collective totems on the one hand, and individual totems and ancestral guardians on the other, was that the former were part of a person's civil status; they were inherited and obligatory rather than acquired on a voluntary basis (Durkheim o.c.: 161-164).

Durkheim was careful to explain that the individualistic potential of these personal cults was inherently limited, because they derived from and had to remain in conformity with the collective cult of which they were but the individualized form (Durkheim o.c.: 280, 325). On the other hand, and perhaps somewhat incongruously, we are also told that individual totemism, despite its optional character, has a much greater potential for survival than collective totemism (Durkheim o.c.: 164).

There is one passage in his book where Durkheim makes more or less explicit that individual cults are to be seen as an emergent form of the modern cult of the individual. Referring to beliefs in the personal soul, individual totems and protecting ancestors, he declares:

> "these beings are the objects of rites which the individual can celebrate by himself, outside of any group; this is the first form of the individual cult. To be sure, it is only a rudimentary cult; but since the personality of the individual is only slightly marked, and but little value is attributed to it, the cult which expresses it could hardly be expected to developed as yet. But as individuals have developed more and more and the value of an individual has increased, the corresponding cult has taken a relatively greater place in the totality of the religious life..." (Durkheim o.c.: 424-425).

If we are correct in interpreting Durkheim as saying that the individual cults of the Australian tribesmen are to be viewed as primeval manifestations of the cult of the individual, we are once again facing a problem, for, in terms of his own definitions, these two forms of religion are radically different. Individual cults, as we have seen, are cults which continue to affirm the sacredness of the human group. The cult of the individual, on the other hand, though necessarily collective, denies the human group - whatever group, except the totality of mankind - any claim to sacredness and religious status. There can be countless individual cults, but there can only be one cult of the individual. Durkheim should have made it one of his tasks to find out what it is that urges human beings to affirm their own worth against that of the group to which they belong, but he never attempts this in his account of Australian religion. Instead, he makes every possible effort, by means of evolutionist hypothesizing and doubtful theologizing, to establish that, after all, individual cults are little more than a particular facet of the cult of the group.

Durkheim also failed to investigate the possible connections between the universalistic and individualistic tendencies in totemic religion. He came close to doing so in the concluding section of his book, when he wrote: "But if religion is the product of social causes, how can we explain the individual cult and the universalistic character of certain religions?" (Durkheim o.c.: 424). In his answer to that question, however, he continues to discuss universalism and individualism as separate issues. This is the more surprising, as he had already mentioned their interrelation in his writings on modern morality, when positing that the only creed which could lead to a truly universal religion was the cult of the individual (Bellah 1973a:

51). Once again, then, we must conclude that a concept which was quite crucial to his theory of religion, was left unanalyzed.

3.3 Real or ideal society?

In his summarizing section, Durkheim also asks himself the question which society is being venerated in religion (Durkheim 1915: 420-422). "Is it actual society with all its imperfections, in which evil goes beside the good, injustice often reigns supreme, and the truth is often concealed by error? Or is it some ideal society, entirely different from the real one?" If the latter should be the case, the objection might be made that it is not social experience but some preconceived idea which gives rise to religion. Durkheim replies that neither conception is correct, for religion is an enlarged, transformed and idealized conception of social reality, both under its positive and negative aspects. "It knows powers of good and evil, of light and darkness, and if we see that in the majority of cases the good triumphs, it is because reality is not otherwise".

Let us consider this statement more closely. What Durkheim seems to be saying is that what is considered morally good in society is represented on the religious plane by such beings as God and auspicious spirits, whereas what is considered morally bad is symbolized by such beings as the devil and evil spirits. The very fact that this kind of distinction is universal should be proof that no society sees itself as perfect and worthy of unqualified self-worship. In other words, all societies have their imperfections, and they know it. This in fact is one of the guiding principles in his discussion of what he called negative cult and piacular rites. Still, his argument seems to contain a basic flaw. Let us take for our example an extreme case of political religion. Such a religion also has its angels and devils, its saints and its sinners. Expressed differently, it also defines what is good and what is bad, but it is precisely on this ground that it justifies all manner of internal oppression and external aggression. Distinguishing between good and bad is therefore not enough; what matters are the criteria on the basis of which such a distinction is made. Durkheim's answer therefore does not solve the problem; it only obscures it.

3.4 Durkheim's conception of civil religion

Durkheim's thinking on modern religion moved in two directions which he described as national and universal respectively. At the present stage, national religion, or civil religion as it has come to be called since the publication of Bellah's articles, was still necessary, but there seemed to be indications that it would soon be superseded by a religion of mankind which centred on the autonomy of the individual. Still, even before this would have become a fact, national religion had to include universalist elements, if it was not to become a dangerous form of national self-worship. Durkheim thought he saw this happening in the case of Germany at the time of the First World War. Germany, so he wrote, was returning to a sort of pagan morality, which assumed that humanity was confined to the tribe (Wallace 1977: 288). It is interesting and I think revealing, that tribal religion which in one context aroused Durkheim's admiration, was here being referred to as something objectionable. We may at this point consider another statement, this time from a letter written by Durkheim's nephew and disciple Marcel Mauss, in which he reflects on the rise of modern political religion:

"One thing that, fundamentally, we never foresaw was how many large modern societies, that have more or less emerged from the Middle Ages in other respects, could be hypnotized like Australians are by their dances, and set in motion like a children's roundabout. This return to the primitive had not been the object of our thoughts. We contented ourselves with several allusions to crowd situations, while it was a question of something quite different. We also contented ourselves with proving that it was in the collective mind that the individual could find the basis and sustenance of his liberty, his independence and his criticism. Basically, we never allowed for the extraordinary new possibilities... I believe that all this is a real tragedy for us, too powerful a verification of things that we had indicated and the proof that we should have expected this verification through evil rather than a verification through goodness" (Lukes 1975: 339).

Mauss' letter is of considerable importance as it comes from someone who was very close to Durkheim. It may therefore be instructive to have a closer look at its contents.

First, Mauss, like Durkheim, sees modern nationalism as a 'return to the primitive', which he specifies as a proclivity to mass hypnosis on the occasion of communal celebrations. Modern nationalists, like Australian primitives, seem to lose their critical faculties when finding themselves in crowd situations.

Second, the letter seems to suggest that Durkheim and his folowers had used primitive crowd situations to prove or illustrate 'something quite different' from what modern nationalist crowds exhibited.

Mauss does not specify what this 'something different' was, but this may be inferred from Durkheim's own writings in which tribal celebrations are invariably described as generating and regenerating social consciousness in the non-objectionable sense.

Third, it is maintained that the Durkheimians had conceived of the collective mind (Mauss uses the term *esprit collectif*) as the source of the individual's liberty, independence, personality and criticism (*critique*), whereas the effects of the modern nationalist ideology appear to be the opposite. I must confess surprise at seeing the word 'criticism' appear in this context, for it would be difficult to discover a passage in Durkheim's description of primitive life or primitive religion in which he allows for criticism or protest.

Fourth, it is said that modern nationalism is to be regarded as a verification of Durkheim's theory of religion, be it in an unexpected and profoundly objectionable sense. Lukes quotes yet another Durkheimian, Leon Brunschvicg, as having expressed the same feeling, when he said that Nuremberg was religion in the Durkheimian sense of society adoring itself (Lukes *ibid*).

It will not be difficult to agree with Mauss' final statement that to the Durkheimians this was a tragedy they had never expected. Durkheim's theory of religion had been vindicated, not as the blueprint for civilized society which he had developed in his lectures on moral education, but in a quite different and utterly evil sense. That discovery surprised and disconcerted Mauss, but it did not lead him - at least not in the letter just quoted - to question the theory itself or its underlying assumptions. Yet, both he and Durkheim could have found the beginning of an answer to their problem, if they had asked themselves why they had such ambiguous feelings about Australian religion. Durkheim had always maintained that it should be considered as the proto-type of all religion, for it contained within itself all that the great religions possessed, up to and including an 'international orientation'. But when he was confronted with the realities of German nationalism, the same religion became the proto-type of narrow nationalism. Whence this inconsistency? One possible answer would be that Durkheim's view of Australian religion had changed after the publication of *The Elementary Forms of the Religious Life* in 1912. It seems more likely though that the ambiguity had been there all along, and that the war situation had brought it into the open. My own suggestion would be that Durkheim's ambivalent view of Australian tribal society and Australian religion is to be regarded as a faithful reflection of his ambivalent view of the modern nation. Let me explain myself.

It is well known, and we have had occasion to mention this at an earlier stage, that Durkheim's writings on morality, religion and education had for their most immediate aim the uplift of the French nation. We find this clearly expressed in his essay "The School of Tomorrow", where he outlines the task of the public school as follows:

"The end is not difficult to discover: It is the moral greatness of France. Our whole teaching should develop around this idea: to awaken the corresponding feeling, implant it in all the hearts, and cultivate it as far as possible. Such would be the chief task of the school" (Wallace 1977: 80).

The nation was for Durkheim the social unit in which secular religion was to be realized first and foremost. Correspondingly, his conception of the nation was that of a religious congregation, united on the basis of one creed and one cult. He had outlined that creed in his lectures on moral education, and in the same treatise he had detailed how it was to be instilled in the younger generation. As we have suggested before, one of the keys to an adequate understanding of Durkheim's thinking is his view, never explicitly stated but always implicitly present, that the Australian clan was the proto-type of the modern nation. It is my suggestion, then, that the clan, insofar as it provided the model for a viable nation and a healthy patriotism, was attributed the positive connotations which are found all through his writings on primitive religion. Nation, nationhood and patriotism, however, could also manifest themselves in a less innocuous form, which is what Durkheim became painfully aware of in the case of Germany. I suggest, then, that it was this experience which may have led him to view the clan and its religion in a negative manner. It was a strange way of saying farewell to something that had occupied his thoughts and inspired his most influential writings for close to twenty years, but it was necessary, because his conception of clan religion had become exposed for the ambiguous concept it was. When Durkheim reached that stage, he could have done one sensible thing, which was to apply the same insight to his conception of civil religion. Instead, he applied it to German nationalism, and there it ended. It may seem to some that I am reading too much into a couple of statements that Durkheim made in his last years. If such is the case, I stand open to correction, but it can be no coincidence that Mauss, Durkheim's closest collaborator, drew the same conclusion as Durkheim; only more explicitly so.

Having come to this point, I would like to suggest that Durkheim had already developed a number of concepts which, had he been able to integrate them in his theory of religion more fully than he did, might have opened up fresh lines of analysis. One of these concepts is his 'cult of the individual', which found its earliest expression in his book on the social division of labour, published in 1893, and which reappears with a certain regularity in his later writings. In the 1893 work, Durkheim, after having observed that in modern industrial societies the domain of religion contracts more and more, and that there is an ever decreasing number of collective beliefs and sentiments that are both collective enough and strong enough to take on a religious character, allows for one exception - that is the way it regards the individual who becomes the object of a sort of religion (Lukes 1975: 156). Five years later, at the time of the Dreyfuss Affair, he was to write:

> "The human person, whose definition serves as the touchstone according to which good must be distinguished from evil, is considered as sacred, in what one might call the ritual sense of the word. It has something of that transcendental majesty which the churches of all times have given to their God. It is conceived as being invested with that mysterious property which creates an empty space around holy objects, which keeps them away from profane contacts and which draws them away from ordinary life. And it is exactly this feature which induces the respect of which it is the object. Whoever makes an attempt on a man's life, on a man's liberty, on a man's honour, inspires us with a feeling of horror in every way analogous to that which the believer experiences when he sees his idol profaned. Such a morality is therefore not simply a hygienic discipline or a wise principle of economy. It is a religion of which man is, at the same time, both believer and God". (Lukes o.c.: 340-341).

What is of importance to our argument is that Durkheim sees this cult of the individual as replacing other religions, including civil religions. It is a religion which addresses itself to all humanity:

> "After all, individualism... is the glorification not of the self but of the individual in general. It springs not from egoism but from sympathy for all that is human, a broader pity for all sufferings, for all human miseries, a more ardent need to combat them and mitigate them, a greater thirst for justice. Is there not herein what is needed to place all men of good will in communion?" (Bellah 1973a: 48-9).

The second element that we must pay attention to is Durkheim's conception of the state as developed in his political lectures, given between 1898 and 1900. There, he asserts that the growth of individualism is dependent on the growth of the democratic state. This is so, because it has been able to contain the tyrannical authority of families, guilds and 'coteries of every kind' which have oppressed the individual. But if the state is to be the liberator of the individual, some counterbalance is necessary; it must be restrained by secondary groups appropriate to the structure of modern society, for it is out of this conflict of social forces that individual liberties are born (Bellah o.c.: xxxiii-xxiv). However, the state is not only the protector of individual rights, it also has the duty "to organize the cult, to be the head of it, and to ensure its regular working and development" (Bellah o.c.: xxv). Here, Durkheim seems to be skating on thin ice, for the state is assigned a role for which, as we have argued when discussing American civil religion, it is not equipped, since it will always tend to give national values priority over universal values and to interpret national values as universal values. Durkheim offers a way to reconcile the tension:

> "That is, for the national to merge with the human ideal, for the individual States to become, each in their own way, the agencies by which this general idea is carried into effect. If each State had as its chief aim, not to expand, or to lengthen its borders, but to set its own house in order and to make the widest appeal to its members for a moral life on an ever higher level, then all discrepancy between national and human morals would be excluded. If the state had no other purpose than making men of its citizens, in the widest sense of the term, then civil duties would be only a particular form of the general obligations of humanity" (Bellah o.c.: xxv-xxvi).

In sum, then, Durkheim's view of religion in modern society combines patriotic values with universal values in a way which seems to him perfectly satisfactory. If only the various nations would mend their ways, all problems would disappear. But nations seldom mend their ways, and narrow nationalism is a fact of life. Once again, Durkheim's error has been to take the nation for the basic unit in which modern religion has to come to life, and this error is only compounded by putting the state in charge of it. No combination could be more disastrous in a world which is trying to establish effective international relations and an effective international consciousness. What the world needs least at this juncture is states which see themselves as providers of religion. The sensible thing to do right now is divest the state of any ambition of this kind. Durkheim would have been more in tune with reality, if he had written off national religion as an outdated concept. Bellah calls him "a high priest and theologian of the civil religion of the Third Republic and a prophet calling not only to modern France but modern western society generally to mend its ways in the face of a great social and moral crisis" (Bellah o.c.: x). No description could more aptly bring out the two sides of Durkheim. As a priest he fulfilled an essentially conservative role in maintaining the rituals of the national cult and the harmonious life of its community. As a prophet he tried to relativize that same cult in an effort to bring national communities together. Few if any individuals are able fully to harmonize these two vocations. Durkheim at any rate did not succeed, as he tried to do too much with a conception of religion that was too narrow. What he needed but did not manage to formulate was a dialectical conception of religion in which not only its particularizing tendencies - as evidenced by civil religion - but also its universalizing tendencies - as evidenced by his cult of the individual - would be given their full due. It is suggested that V. W. Turner has opened the way to this kind of thinking, and it is to him that we shall therefore turn in our final section.

Turner's Structure and Communitas 4.

In his book *The Ritual Process* Turner develops the idea that the social is not to be regarded as being identical only with the social-structural. Beyond the structural lies not just the Hobbesian 'war of all against all', but something else to which he gives the name of communitas. Structure and communitas are two contrasting social models.

> "One... is of society as a structure of jural, political and economic positions, offices, statuses and roles, in which the individual is only ambiguously grasped behind the social persona. The other is of society as a communitas of concrete idiosyncratic individuals, who, though differing in physical and mental endowment, are nevertheless regarded as equal in terms of shared humanity. The first model is of a differentiated, culturally structured, segmented, and often hierarchical system of institutionalized positions. The second presents society as an undifferentiated, homogeneous whole, in which individuals confront another integrally and not as 'segmentalized into statuses and roles' (Turner 1974: 166).

As stated, the relation between communitas and structure is one of opposites: "communitas emerges where social structure is not" and communitas can be viewed as 'anti-structure' (Turner o.c.: 113). They are two major models for human interrelatedness, juxtaposed and alternating (Turner o.c.: 82). There can be no structure without communitas, for communitas is "a matter of giving recognition to an essential and generic human bond without which there could be *no* society" (Turner o.c.: 83). Elsewhere he states that "structural action swiftly becomes arid and mechanical if those involved in it are not periodically immersed in the regenerative abyss of communitas" (Turner o.c.: 127). On the other hand, there can be no communitas without structure, for communitas is made evident or accessible only through its juxtaposition to, or hybridization with, aspects of social structure (Turner o.c.: 114). From these various observations he draws the conclusion that "social life is a type of dialectical process that involves successive experience of high and low, communitas and structure, homogeneity and differentiation, equality and inequality. In other words, each individual's life experience contains alternating exposure to structure and communitas (Turner o.c.: 83). In Turner's view

> "no society can function adequately without this dialectic, for exaggeration of structure may well lead to pathological manifestations of communitas outside or against 'the law'. Exaggeration of communitas, in certain religious or political movements of the levelling type, may be speedily followed by despotism, overbureaucratization, or other modes of structural rigidification... Communitas cannot stand alone if the material and organisational needs of human beings are to be adequately met. Maximisation of communitas provokes maximisation of structure, which in its turn produces revolutionary strivings for renewed communitas" (Turner o.c.: 116).

On what basis does Turner come to this brilliant and novel conception? From his own writings it appears that it was inspired, among other things, by his study of the initiation rituals among the Ndembu of present-day Zambia. It had struck him that the period of exclusion - or, in Van Gennep's terminology, the liminal phase of these rituals - was characterized by such attributes as anonimity, equality, absence of rank, nakedness, sexual continence, humility, disregard for personal appearance, unselfishness, silence, simplicity and acceptance of suffering (Turner o.c.: 92-93). The same or similar attributes were noticed in other Ndembu rituals such as those accompanying the installation of a chief. More generally, one may observe them in a great many rites of passage among primitive peoples and, in a permanently institutionalized form, among religious orders within the Christian, Buddhist and Hindu tradition.

The meaning of these attributes of liminality is made clear in his analysis of the Ndembu enthronement ritual, where he states that its aim is to imbue the future chief with the generic bond of communitas. He must not keep the chieftaincy to himself for he is ultimately an ordinary human being. One of the more striking aspects of this ritual is that the person in charge of his phase of the ritual is the Kafwana, who is the head of an autochthonous people which became subjected to the Ndembu in the course of time. Being the representative of what in fact amounts to an inferior social group, he is the bearer of the principle of communitas. Again, this fact does not stand by itself, for Turner reminds us that socially inferior groups and persons are often considered to have special religious or ritual power. This is 'the power of the weak', the central conception in I. M. Lewis' *Ecstatic Religion* (Lewis 1971). The same theme may be observed in the fact that the female line in patrilineally organized societies and the male line in matrilineal organisations are often credited with this 'power of the weak', while they are also bearers of the idea of communitas (Turner o.c.: 100-112). It is also a recurrent theme in folk-literature which abounds in 'holy beggars', 'third sons', 'little tailors' and 'simpletons' who strip off the pretentions of holders of high rank and office and reduce them to the level of common humanity and mortality (Turner o.c.: 100).

However, it is not only the socially inferior but also the socially marginal who may act as the representatives of the principle of communitas. Such marginality is particularly characteristic of the monastic orders in the various traditions. The Christian monks for instance try to express the adagium that the Christian is a stranger to the world, a pilgrim, a traveller, with no place to rest his head (Turner o.c.: 93). Their existence is a protest against social structure as 'the world', i.e. institutionalized sin, which the Christian should avoid. Buddhist and Hindu monks denounce the existing structure as an appearance, the world of those who do not know man's real situation. Again, there are countless variations on this theme, such as the life style of the beat generation and the hippies (Turner o.c.: 99). All these phenomena share attributes which are characteristic of communitas and, however different they may be, all have in common that they are persons or principles that fall in the interstices of social structure, are on its margins, or occupy its lowest rungs (Turner o.c.: 112). Elsewhere, the same thing is phrased differently, when it is said that communitas breaks in through the interstices of structure in liminality; at the edges of structure, in marginality; and from beneath structure in inferiority (Turner o.c.: 115).

Turner makes two further points which are of direct relevance to the argument of this paper. The first is the observation that communitas (or rather its various manifestations) is almost everywhere held to be sacred or holy; the second is the observation that, from the viewpoint of those concerned with the maintenance of structure, all sustained manifestation of communitas must appear as dangerous and anarchical (Turner o.c.: 95). The reason for both these reactions may be that communitas transgresses and dissolves the norms that govern structured and institutionalized relationships and is accompanied by manifestations of unprecedented potency (Turner o.c.: 115). This does not mean, however, that structure cannot be sacralized. It often is, and certain fixed offices in tribal societies have many sacred attributes. The sacred, then, moves between structure and anti-structure.

4.1 *Durkheim and Turner*

There appear to be a number of elements in Turner's concepts of structure and communitas that are of direct relevance to Durkheim's theory of religion. Thus it is said that religion may not only sanction structure but also its opposite, anti-structure. It also appears that primitive religion and ritual contain moments in which not the value of the group but the value of the individual is emphasized. Finally, it is suggested that by 'ideal society' we need not only understand actual society minus its imperfections, but also actual society minus every form of differentiation. We shall discuss these three aspects in turn beginning with the last one mentioned.

Durkheim's seminal insight that God is to be regarded as a symbol of society raised the question: Which society? Is it actual society with all its imperfections, or is it some ideal condition? Aron maintains that, if the former is the case, religion would be the essence of impiety. On the other hand, if the divine symbol would refer to an ideal conception, religion could no longer be interpreted as originating from social experience (Aron 1970: 67-68). We have seen that Durkheim formulated much the same dilemma, which he thought he had solved by positing that all religions distinguished between good and bad, and that no religion considered the society in which it was grounded as free from evil. That solution, however, was shown to be unsatisfactory, as it did not consider the criteria according to which the good and the bad were to be identified. Thus a society could define as morally good whatever contributed to its survival, no matter the amount of oppression and agression that might be involved. Durkheim, of course, never meant his proposition to be interpreted that way, for when he spoke of the morally good, he undoubtedly understood it as being in conformity with universal values. Still, even Durkheim's universal values may not be as universal as their name implies, for primitive societies are said to be only vaguely aware of them, and the concept is so broad as to allow for quite divergent interpretations. Turner's conception of ideal society as anti-structure is much more radical, as its formulation of what is to be considered 'good' does not - at least not in essence - vary from culture to culture and from situation to situation. It is the same for all cultures, for the 'good' is defined as the absence of differentiation, any form of differentiation. Turner brings this out quite clearly by drawing his examples from every kind of society, primitive and modern, eastern and western. His theory also answers, or so it appears to this writer - Aron's objection that the concept of ideal society cannot be rooted in actual experience, for if social differentiation is an experiential fact, so is its negation. It seems therefore legitimate to state that Turner's concepts allow us to interpret Durkheim's thesis that God is to be considered as a symbol of society in two senses, which are each other's polar opposites. God may be a symbol of structure, by which is meant everything that has to do with social differentiation; and God may be a symbol of anti-structure or the negation of differentiation. Both modes of symbolization seem verified by empirical reality.

Let us now consider the relationship between the individual and society in the light of the same concepts. We have noticed Durkheim's problem in this respect. In primitive society, the individual was so to speak indistinguishable from the community. In the society of the future he would be entirely autonomous and himself the object of religious worship. In the present situation he found himself somewhere mid-way between these two positions. The group as constituted by the nation was still important, important enough to have a cult of its own, but the nation had also for one of its tasks to bring the cult of the individual into being and thus make itself ultimately redundant as a religious unit.

Turner appears to complement and modify this view in several ways. He shows for instance that individualism, very much in the sense in which Durkheim defined it, is at the root of all religion, including primitive religion. Durkheim was rather uncertain on this point. He saw it as a later development and as something which manifested itself as it were on the fringe of primitive society in such concepts as personal totems and guardian spirits. Turner on the other hand, quite firmly places it in the centre of primitive religion as the manifestation of anti-structure. Had Durkheim been aware of this, he would not have compared Australian religion with German nationalist manifestations, for he would have been able to perceive the difference between them. German nationalism was the glorification of structure in an unmitigated sense, while Australian religion was not.

Turner could also have helped solve Durkheim's problem of

accounting for the universalizing tendency in religion. It will be recalled that Durkheim had considerable difficulty in explaining how clan religion could become tribal and intertribal or 'international'. His solution was that this had come about as an effect of a widening of the social scale, but he never made clear how clan identity could be reconciled with a wider social identity. Turner's theory suggests that religion universalizes on the basis of anti-structure and individualism, for it is anti-structure which negates differentiation of whatever kind. It is therefore no coincidence that Durkheim equated universal religion with individualism. It was empirical observation as much as intuition and logic, which led him to this position.

There is also a sense, and maybe an important sense, in which Durkheim complements Turner. For one thing, Durkheim, in his discussions of individualism, gives us one of the clearest and, it should be added, least utopian formulations of what Turner rather unfortunately calls 'ideological communitas'. But Durkheim does more than that. Where Turner sees communitas in modern industrial society as manifested mainly in incidental or marginal situations, Durkheim sees it as moving into the very centre of modern consciousness. It is at this point that Durkheim the priest truly makes way for Durkheim the prophet.

Concluding remarks 5.

In this essay we have tried to demonstrate that Durkheim's theory of religion contains an ambiguity, which is at the base of the often repeated criticism that it was an exercise in nation worship. Durkheim's defenders have always pointed out that this was a gross misrepresentation of his real views, for far from idolizing the nation, he had always insisted that national values had to be in accordance with universal values. In actual fact this cleared Durkheim only of the charge of having constructed his theory of religion with objectionable intentions. The charge that the theory itself could be interpreted in a nationalist sense remained unanswered. Part of the problem was that there existed no empirical study to which the critics might refer, since Durkheim's empirical work on religion had confined itself to primitive societies. That gap has in the meantime been filled by R. N. Bellah's study of American civil religion, which may well be one of the finest pieces of Durkheimian analysis in existence. Bellah has, knowingly or unknowingly, put Durkheim's ideas to the test. As we have seen, it evoked, quite independently, the same criticisms and the same charges that were made against Durkheim. Like Durkheim, Bellah defended himself by stating that the religious complex he had described contained the very principles necessary to protect it from becoming a form of 'American Shinto'. Yet, his critics were not convinced, and rightly so, for it was evident that American civil religion, despite its belief in universal values, could hardly be called a national religion, as large sections of the population found it impossible to identify with it. Some even went as far as seeing in it a justification for internal oppression and external aggressiveness. The Marxist writer Paul Nizan had expressed essentially the same feeling, when he said that through Durkheim's influence "teachers taught children to respect the French nation, to justify class collaboration, to accept everything, to join in the cult of the Flag and bourgeois Democracy" (Lukes 1975: 357). Bellah clearly saw this, but he saw these negative effects not as something that followed from the concept of civil religion. Rather, they were to be attributed to the errors made by those who were responsible for its proper functioning. It is this particular argument which we have tried to disprove in the present essay by positing that the sacralization of a nation, inescapably leads to consequences which are irreconcilable with a fully democratic state system.

Durkheim has rendered us the invaluable service of showing in the most consistent and penetrating manner how group sacralization works and how it contributes to the integration of a society, but he did not pay sufficient attention to its negative effects and to the social mechanisms, which operate against it. It has been suggested that V. W. Turner's concepts of structure and anti-structure constitute a vital contribution in precisely this field, for he has shown that religion may sacralize and desacralize, affirm and negate the principle of differentiation on which human groups organize themselves, and on the basis of which they construct their identity. Turner has broken new ground and, by so doing, has placed Durkheim in sharper perspective.

Acknowledgement
I am grateful to Mrs. Sylvia Broere-Moore for her helpful comments on the text and to Professor Hans Tennekes for allowing me to make free use of one of his seminar papers on V. W. Turner.

Bibliography

Apter, David E.
   1963 Political Religion in the New Nations. *In* Old Societies and New States. C. Geertz, ed. Pp. 57-104. New York: The Free Press.

Aron, Raymond
   1970 Main Currents in Sociological Thought. Vol. 2. Harmondsworth: Penguin.

Bellah, Robert N.
   1957 Tokugawa Religion. New York: The Free Press.

Bellah, Robert N.
   1970 Civil Religion in America. *In* Beyond Belief; Essays on Religiom in a Post-Traditional World. Pp. 168-189. New York: Harper & Row.

Bellah, Robert N.
   1973a Emile Durkheim on Morality and Society. Chicago: The University of Chicago Press.

Bellah, Robert N.
   1973b American Civil Religion in the 1970's. Anglican Theological Review, Supplementary Series 1: 8-20.

Durkheim, Emile
   1915 The Elementary Forms of the Religious Life. London: George Allen & Unwin.

Durkheim, Emile
   1973 Moral Education; A Study in the Theory and Application of the Sociology of Education. New York: The Free Press.

Lewis, I. M.
   1971 Ecstatic Religion; An Anthropological Study of Spirit Possession and Shamanism. Harmondsworth: Penguin.

Lukes, Steven
   1975 Emile Durkheim: His Life and Work. Harmondsworth: Penguin.

Parsons, Talcott
   1973 Durkheim on Religion Revisited: Another Look at the Elementary Forms of the Religious Life. *In* Beyond the Classics? Essays in the Scientific Study of Religion. C. Glock and Ph. Hammons, eds. Pp. 156-180. New York: Harper & Row.

Turner, Victor W.
   1974 The Ritual Process. Harmondsworth: Penguin.

Wallace, Ruth A.
   1977 Emile Durkheim and the Civil Religion Concept. Review of Religious Research 18: 287-290.

Singular and plural ethical systems: a critical analysis of the Weber thesis

by Daniel Meijers

Introduction[1]

This paper is an attempt to arrive at a critical appreciation of the Weber thesis. The essential question the writer asks himself is: if the development of modern capitalism must necessarily be linked to innerworldly asceticism: *innerweltliche Askese*. The Portuguese Jews in Holland, in the post Reformation era, are used as an example, and it is shown that they were not ascetic but that the signs of a modern, capitalistic development can, nevertheless, be observed in them. In addition, a number of Oriental religions are examined.

It is concluded that there are other conditions required to arrive at a modern capitalism in the Weberian sense. It is suggested that the form, as well as the content, of the ethical or religious system is of importance. If there were more than óne ethical system in one group, optimum meaningful life would be impossible, because any one system will deprive the other of its value. Making it impossible for man to act rationally: a prerequisite for modern capitalism. Only when a group has óne ethical system is it possible for the members of that group to lead optimum meaningful lives and to act rationally.

The Weber thesis 1.

The Weber thesis postulates a link between the ethic of Protestantism and the spirit of capitalism. The Protestant ethic evokes an attitude which leads to a specific way of economic behaviour, i.e. the behaviour belonging to modern capitalism. In order properly to understand this theme, we will outline both the Protestant ethic as well as examine what Weber means by modern capitalism.

1.1 The Protestant ethic

The Protestant ethic is characterised by a dogma of predestination: it has been laid down whether or not man will be among the elect. Thereby the elect, only, are capable of moral achievements - for moral achievement is not a means to being elected, but evidence of election. From this, it follows that the believer will make an effort to arrive at a mode of living which proves - most especially to himself - that he belongs to the elect. One inherent part of this mode of living is an ascetic attitude. Through this attitude he can attain salvation, but once again governed by the restriction that the attitude in question is experienced by the believers themselves as a sign and not as a means to an end.

> Salvation may be viewed as the distinctive gift of active ethical behavior performed in the awareness that G-d directs this behavior, i.e. that the actor is an instrument of G-d. We shall designate this type of attitude toward salvation, which is characterized by a methodical procedure for achieving religious salvation, as "ascetic" (Weber 1965: 164).[1A]

Weber has termed the specific form which asceticism has acquired in Protestantism: *innerweltliche Askese* or innerworldly asceticism.

> ..., the unique concentration of human behavior on activities leading to salvation may require the participation within the world (or more precisely: within the institutions of the world but in opposition to them) of the religious individual's idiosyn-

cratically sacred religious mood and his qualifications as the elect instrument of G-d. This is inner-worldly asceticism (Weber 1965: 166).

This form of asceticism demands the utmost self-discipline, which results in methodical procedures in acting.

G-d is to be served, and since such service cannot consist in indulgence of or adaptation to the things of the flesh, it must consist in their disciplined control: this is the meaning of "inner-worldly asceticism" (Hill 1973: 110).

This systematic, methodical element, which innerworldly asceticism brings with it, extends to all spheres of life and makes acting - even each separate action - meaningful. Because each action demands meaning and justification, the systematic element is the basis of a certain form of action, i.e. rational action[2].

In the economic sphere too, a rational attitude is highly important for business achievements which are not based purely on speculation. It is this rational attitude which, according to Weber, is so characteristic of early Protestantism and has remained an essential element of Protestant thinking. Hence the relationship to modern capitalism.

The "spirit of capitalism" must not exclusively be considered a logical consequence of the ascetic attitiude of the Puritans. It has deeper roots. Nonetheless, Puritan asceticism has been an impelling force towards a rationality important to the form of capitalism as described by Weber.

Another important factor is the Puritan concept of success in business. Just as moral achievement is a sign of being elected rather than the means thereto, success in one's occupation is a sign of Divine favour (Weber 1965: 167). This results in an effort to succeed in business. Capitalistic success then raises a person's status, for it is a sign of Divine Mercy (Gerth & Mills 1966: 322). It becomes a question of moral justification of worldly activities, which Weber considers one of the most important results of the Reformation (Weber 1958: 81). In line with this, Weber remarks that both the German word *Beruf* and the English word "calling" have a religious connotation, i.e. a task created by G-d (Weber 1958: 79).

Consequently, the occupation must be practised in an ethical manner. This led to Protestant groups becoming renowned for their honest business dealings. People therefore liked doing business with them.

Another point which needs to be emphasized here and which will prove to be important to what we want to show, is Weber's finding that Puritanism also distinguished itself from the Catholic Middle Ages in that there was little difference between clergymen and laymen. In contrast to the Middle Ages, where the ethic of religious orders was other than that of laymen, Puritanism distinguishes itself from Catholicism by having a singular ethical system. The church was partly, if not wholly, in the hands of laymen (Gerth & Mills 1966: 320). The majority of Protestant sects did not have a professional clergyman at their disposal (Weber 1964: 239).

The link that Weber sees between the Protestant ethic and the spirit of capitalism is made plausible by his examples of Protestant settlements and the subsequent development of capitalism. Such is the case in Pennsylvania, where a number of German immigrants settle. There is also a difference to be observed in places settled by Huguenots and by others (Weber 1958: 39, 43, 75; Bendix 1962: 56). All this leads to the supposition of there being a connection between the ethic of Protestantism and the spirit of capitalism.

1.2 *Capitalism and modern capitalism*

When Weber speaks of the spirit of capitalism, he associates it with modern capitalism as opposed to traditional forms of capitalism. After all, there were forms of capitalism to be noted prior to the Reformation and these occurred in countries without Protestant groups. Weber speaks of Western capitalism as contrasted to Oriental forms of capitalism and of modern capitalism as contrasted to the capitalism of the Middle Ages. He also speaks of modern, Western capitalism, which shows that he is dealing with one and the same contrast. According to Weber, however, this modern form first came into being after the Reformation. The question now arises just what Weber meant by capitalistic enterprise generally, and then examine in which way his definition differs from modern capitalism.

> The impulse to acquisition, pursuit of gain, of money of the greatest possible amount of money, has in itself nothing to do with capitalism... But capitalism is identical with the pursuit of profit, and forever renewed profit, by means of continuous, rational, capitalistic enterprise. ...We will define a capitalistic economic action as one which rests on the expectation of profit by the utilization of opportunities for exchange, that is on (formally) peaceful chances of profit (Weber 1958: 17).

So this capitalism can assume different forms. Modern capitalism which, for instance, knows industrial activities, is quite different from the various kinds of profit-making which, at an earlier date, represented the major sources of income, such as the profits from colonialism, raising of tribute etc. The characteristic feature of modern capitalism is, on the contrary, "the rational capitalistic organization of (formally) free labour" (Weber 1958: 21). The essence of modern capitalism is the role played by rational acts, which are not based merely on speculation.

> Modern capitalism is a great complex of interrelated institutions based on rational rather than speculative types of economic pursuit. In particular this complex involves enterprises that are based on long-range capital investments, a voluntary supply of labor in the legal senses of that word, a planned division of labor within the enterprises, and an allocation of production functions among them through the operation of a market economy. Only under capitalism do we find, furthermore, the legal form of the business corporation, organized exchanges for trading in commodities and securities, and the organization of enterprises for the production of goods rather than merely for trade in goods (Bendix 1962: 53-54).

The capitalistic entrepreneur too is characterized by a certain attitude:

> The indispensable ethical qualities of the modern capitalist entrepreneur were: radical concentration on Gd-ordained purposes; the relentless and practical rationalism of the ascetist ethic; a methodical conception of matter-of-factness in business management; a horror of illegal, political, colonial, booty, and monopoly types of capitalism which depended on the favor of princes and men as against the sober, strict legality and the harnessed rational energy of routine enterprise; the rational calculation of the technical best way, of practical solidity and expediency instead of the traditionalist enjoyment of transmitted skill or the beauty of product characteristic of the old artisan craftsman. This must be added to the pious worker's special will for work (Weber 1964: 247).

One might ask if Weber describes the modern capitalist here, or if he gives a description of the Puritan and declares him to be a capitalist!

This comment is of importance to us, since in the latter case it becomes self-evident that he could not find a similar development anywhere else. The quote from Bendix is a rather more general one and does not, basically, assume a relationship to the specific attitude which Weber describes. It is quite possible, for instance, to imagine a secularised capitalistic entrepreneur in whom the main data from both quotes are united: a hard-working and above all industrious entrepreneur who sticks to the rules of the game - the traditional firm with the well-established good name, with the rationality, however, which can adapt its business approach to the times and which is geared more towards production than trade. This last distinction has apparently been introduced to fit the rise of industry into the framework of modern capitalism. Although this is undoubtedly a characteristic of modern capitalism, industry by itself cannot serve as a criterium. Characteristics which can likewise be seen as criteria are more likely to be ethics-based hard work in contrast to the more subjective concept of making time meaningful, as well as the formal rationality which appears to be typical of all modern capitalism[3]. Other important elements are a rational accounting system - essential to methodical profit-making - and the division between business and housekeeping (Hill 1973: 126; Bendix 1962: 51-52; Weber 1958: 21-22). The difference, however, between modern capitalism and its more traditional forms appears to be rational action. This last term plays a part in all the references quoted!

Judaism and capitalism 2.

Our criticism of Weber will chiefly be demonstrated by comparing what Weber wrote about Judaism with our own findings. We can hardly criticize Weber for being less informed about Judaism than about other world religions. He had to use the data of Protestant scholars of the turn of the century which are now frequently outdated and he did not have the original sources at his disposal, whose true command requires a lifetime of study (Weber 1960: 425). It is therefore hardly surprising that, to our minds, Weber's findings about Judaism in relation to ethics and capitalism do not always have a strong foundation. So we will try, whenever this is the case, to cite other passages from Jewish literature or from the literature about Judaism, which contradict these findings.[4]

2.1 Judaism: traditional or modern capitalism?

The essence of the Weberian description of economic developments in Judaism is that Judaism is indeed characterized by capitalism, but not by the modern capitalism that Weber sees as characteristic of Protestantism (Weber 1965: 248-249). In Weber's opinion, classic Judaism was "largely a religion of traders or financiers" (Weber 1965: 93). In later periods too, he fails to discover a modern capitalistic development:

> This was the organization of industrial production or manufacturing in domestic industry and in the factory system. ...how does one explain the fact that no modern and distinctively industrial bourgeoisie of any significance emerged among the Jews to employ the Jewish workers available for home industry, despite the presence of numerous impecunious artisan groups at almost the threshold of the modern period? (Weber 1965: 249).

In the first place it remains to be seen if Weber is right in saying that classic Judaism largely consisted of traders and financiers. An authority like Ejges points out, for instance, that during certain periods in Jewish Antiquity, Jews concentrated largely on agriculture and, to a lesser extent, on animal husbrandry. In addition to this, he mentions several crafts and even observes that a number of scholars practised a trade as well (Ejges 1930: 9-10). In later times - in the diaspora - Jews are indeed seen to make their living primarily in finance. And this was usually because other sources of livelihood were made inaccessible to them. Even so, a present-day Spanish source reports that in the Middle Ages in Spain, too, Jews engaged in agriculture, although trade probably occupied a more important position (de Quiros 1958: 61, 75-76).[5]

Secondly, one should ask if it is correct to describe the form and manner of acting among Jews as traditionally capitalistic. The situation in Holland in the period after the Reformation is particularly apt here. This period is not only comparable to that in which Weber reports his findings concerning Puritanism, but the Holland of that time was also one of the few regions where Jews were actually enabled to develop their economic capacities. For Holland was an exception to the rule. Jews were admitted more freely than was the case in other countries, and although there were restrictions it can rightly be stated that if Jews were ever enabled to develop modern capitalism, this must have taken place in 16th and 17th century Holland.

The literature mentions several examples which would show that a capitalism was developed in Holland based on formal rationality. In a decree of 1549, issued by Charles V, we read that Marranos - Jews from Spain and Portugal - are told to leave the city of Antwerp. The Antwerp magistrate makes an attempt to reverse the edict. He states that the Marranos have extensively promoted export, and that they drive trade in cotton, sugar, vegetable oils, leather and fruit and market the products of Flemish industry,

> whereby they were satisfied with small profits and less frequently than merchants from others nations suspended their payments... (Dubnow 1927: 426).

In the Remonstrance of Hugo de Groot too, is expressed - in guarded terms - that the presence in Holland of Jews is considered quite important for trade (Meijer 1949: 81, 94, 116). These remarks as such do not necessarily contradict Weber. It may be deducted from them that the Jews occupied a prominent position in the trade of those days. But the question is, if a non-rational capitalism would make a country attempt to retain a certain national group for that country or even - in some cases - to invite them. The Dutch interest for Jews, after all, assumes such proportions that when the Amsterdam Rabbi, Menasshe ben Israel visits Cromwell, the Dutch ambassador in London is asked if he perhaps wants to have Dutch Jews emigrate to England. The government is not satisfied until it learns that Menasshe ben Israel's purpose is the release of his fellow believers in England, who are still suffering from the Inquisition and the matter does not concern Dutch Jews (Sombart 1911: 21-23).[6] Whether or not Gerzon's observation in the Jewish Encyclopedia, that The Netherlands were still a "poor country" prior to the arrival of the Spanish and Portuguese Jews is correct, is possibly going too far (Gerzon 1925: 44). Whatever may be the case, Meijer considers that Sombart's thesis, that the establishment of the Portuguese Jews would have been decisive for Amsterdam's growth into a world trading centre, has been sufficiently disproven (Meijer 1949: 19-20).

It is striking, however, that the Portuguese Jews were considered, by their contemporaries, as important to the economy of a country. Christian IV, the king of Denmark, tried to have Portuguese Jews come to Glückstadt for instance, so as to be able to compete with Hamburg. In 1622 he sent a letter to this effect to the governors of the Portuguese community in Amsterdam with the promise of various rights. The Duke of Savoy arranged the establishment of Portuguese Jews in Nice and the Duke of Modena tried to have them come to Reggio (Da Silva Rosa 1925: 12). This is entirely comparable to the attitude of Frederick William I, who in East Prussia tolerated the Mennonites for being essential to industry, although they refused to participate in military service (Weber 1958: 44). The only difference here is, that in the case of the Portuguese Jews it was a matter of them being invited rather than tolerated.

Another interesting detail is that in the 17th century, a Portuguese Jew wrote a manual for the stock exchange, the first of its kind. Sombart even adds that "up until today it has, in terms of form and content, remained the best description of the stock exchange" (Sombart 1911: 103). We consider that the mention of this manual not only shows that the Jews were active in trade affairs, but did so in an extremely rational way. Otherwise it would hardly be possible to compile a work of such lasting value.

In the third place we wonder if one of Weber's criteria for modern capitalism, i.e. industrialisation, was indeed as impossible to find as Weber takes it to be. In this matter there are also indications that the situation was different than the one presented by Weber. We must again look at 17th century Holland since the Jewish population suffered less from restrictions there than elsewhere.

Despite the resolutions of the States General, which determine that Jews may not at will establish themselves everywhere in Holland (Tal 1898: 54) - which undoubtedly hinders industrialisation - we find industrialisation on a limited scale.

The Israelites were almost everywhere excluded from the guilds. "The Jews, even though they are citizens, may not engage in the trades engaged in by the city's people" stated a charter of the city of Amsterdam in the year 1632. ...In December 1655 a rare exception took place, when a Portuguese Israelite was given permission to start a sugar refinery (Tal 1898: 47).

Because of the charters, the Jews had no access to the flourishing industry. This is why they tried to establish this profitable undertaking in Maarssen, away from charters. Using the water of the river Vecht as a source of energy, they started up a silk mill "intending to cultivate the trade and the progress of crafts in the aforementioned village". It created employment for some 25 inhabitants (ca. 1650 - L.D.M.)... In Amersfoort too, "a certain Portuguese Jew" had in in 1662 installed three "wool weaving-looms" in his house with the mayor's permission and in 1682, Amsterdam citizens, for lack of labour, were forced to have their silk wound outside the city. The Maarssen mill must have flourished and even on Sundays work continued (Zwarts 1922: 14-15).

Zwarts' closing remark echoes Weber's "rastloze Berufsarbeit" (insistent call to work) such as was found among the Protestants. Working on Sundays clearly took the place here of the Saturday, the day of rest.

There were also other branches of industry which developed among the Portuguese Jews. Printing thereby occupied a special position. Through having greater religious freedom and the absence of censorship and also because of the impossibility of achieving anything in a variety of other industrial enterprises because of the existing regulations, this more accessible branch of industry was embraced and made Amsterdam the centre of Hebrew typography. It was of such renown that if one wanted to recommend the beauty of print in a Hebrew work in other countries, it was stated that Amsterdam letters had been used. Amsterdam has therefore known a number of important Hebrew printing houses (Da Silva Rosa 1925: 28-29).

Another industry which assumed considerable proportions was the diamond industry. There were Portuguese-Jewish diamond workers to be found in Amsterdam as early as 1615 (Da Silva Rosa 1925: 31-32). The reason why this industry is so important an example for what we intend to show, is that the diamond industry assumed enormous proportions and was renowned until the Second World War. This makes it clear that, when given the chance, these people liked to engage in industry. The emphasis here should be on "when given the chance", for what set the diamond industry apart was that it was accessible to Jews. There were no restricting regulations because there was no diamond guild!

Weber finding little evidence of industry is therefore no proof of the absence, among Jews of that time, of a modern, capitalistic outlook. One may also put a question mark beside Weber's classification of the Jews of Antiquity as being traditionally capitalistic. There were times in Judaism that trade and financing were not their major activities.

We would in fact like to ask Weber if he would want to stop speaking of a modern capitalistic attitude, should the Protestants, hampered by regulations, not have arrived at industrialisation and have succeeded in trade only. It is obvious that in most cases, the only thing open to Jews was trade. That they tackled this in an extremely rational manner is very obvious as well. Whenever industrialisation was possible they availed themselves of the opportunity. Beyond that it is not unlikely that there was another factor which stood in the way of industrialisation and which is not mentioned by Weber, i.e. that unlike trade it is, of necessity, bound to place. One must own factories and workshops and be personally present. The Jews - and certainly the Portuguese Jews too - have a tradition of persecution behind them. One could be driven away at any moment from one's possessions and dwelling place - something which happened regularly. Therefore industry was not, in the first instance, an attractive proposition. Only in those regions where one felt completely safe was industry ventured upon. Holland is the only existing example of this. That the diamond industry was selected is therefore very understandable. Traditionally, the jewel trade had been an important one among Portuguese Jews, so the product itself was therefore not a new one. And in the event of persecution it was much easier to take to flight with diamonds than with other products. This thought may also, to some extent, have contributed to the development of the diamond industry in Amsterdam. How important the preference for the diamond industry was, also appears from the fact that not only Portuguese Jews were engaged in it, but members of the Ashkenazi community as well (Dubnow 1928: 467).

The diamond industry has, of course, another advantage, which is an essential one in this connection: this work can be done at home (although, certainly later on, large concerns came off the ground). This is also contrary to Weber's ideas about modern capitalism. For the Jews, however, it was important to keep away from the mainstream of social traffic. Even in Holland, where the attitude was comparatively favourable towards Jews, Jews were not permitted to establish themselves everywhere and when they were given permission, their numbers were restricted. Nor was the Christian population allowed to be employed by Jews, although it was permitted the other way around. Jews were prevented from entering public office. The Jewish Nation is not allowed to accept legacies or inheritances, etc. (Meijer 1949: 90-93).

> ...' that a Jew may not witness against a Christian, except in criminal matters, since it is presupposed that all Jews are hereditary enemies of all Christians (Meijer 1949: 108).

It is also incorrect to suppose - something which must be plain from the above - that the Reformation put an end to the discrimination of the Jews, which was such a marked characteristic of the Middle Ages. Men like Luther were anti-semitic in the extreme and his thoughts about the Jews are hardly likely to have had a positive influence on the Protestant sector.[7] The fact that the Jews in Holland experienced more toleration than anywhere else, is not so much a direct consequence of the Reformation but rather the result of the fight for liberty which Dutchmen, on religious grounds, had to conduct against the administration of Philip II, making religious freedom a highly valued element. Added to this was the fact that the Potuguese Jews had fled Spanish rule for exactly the same reasons as those for which Dutchmen had fought.

It can only be seen as rather amazing that despite these regulations and circumstances, we nevertheless learn of industrialisation on a limited scale in The Netherlands of that time. It leads one to suppose that the mentality, which Weber so fiercely denies, was present.

> In any case, the oriental and South and East European regions where the Jews were most and longest at home have failed to develop the specific traits of modern capitalism. This is true of Antiquity as well as of the Middle Ages and modern times (Weber 1960: 345).

In opposition to this we see Jews from the Levant make attempts to get industrialisation on its way in Amsterdam. It is also a known fact that after the arrival of the Jews, trade with Italy and the Levant began to flourish (Tal 1898: 27; Dubnow 1927: 430). Jewish merchants therefore formed part of the Chamber of Amsterdam when the West-Indies Company was established (Tal 1898: 37).

Weber mentioning Eastern Europe is not at all based on accurate information. If there was any place where Jews were limited in their movements and constantly had to be on their guard for pogroms, it was in those particular regions. In this connection, it is rather interesting to note that the leaders of the mystical Chassidic movement kept on attempting, whenever they saw the chance, to improve the material circumstances of the Jews. Through industrialisation among other things. Rabbi Dov Ber of Lubavitch (1774-1828) wrote a letter in which he says that:

> ... strict regulations be introduced in the Jewish communities, whereby the women and children, boys and girls, should learn some basic trades, such as the various types of weaving and spinning, and all skills such as are employed in factories. The training of artisans should likewise be organized... They are also not to despise agriculture. They are to acquire good fertile land, large plots or small, and work the soil... (Outlines 1953: 19).

A descendent of this Chassidic leader, Rabbi J. I. Schneersohn of Lubavitch (1880-1950) established a large industrial concern for spinning and weaving. In this factory in Dubrowna, in the district of Mohilew, 2000 labourers found employment and learned the trade at the same time (Outlines 1953: 34). Consequently we can accept to the full Sombart's statement about the connection between Jews and the modern capitalistic state of mind (in contrast to other thoughts in his work):

> Their significance in the formation of capitalism is so intrinsically important that it may be said that they were responsible for endowing economic life with the modern spirit; for they brought the essence of capitalistic thinking to full development (Sombart 1911: 24).

2.2 *Judaism: the debate between Weber and Sombart*
How can Weber and Sombart arrive at such different conclusion about Judaism? In Weber's opinion, Judaism is capitalistic, but not in the modern sense of that word, whereas Sombart concludes: "Puritanism is Judaism" (Sombart 1911: 293).

Sombart tries to show by comparing Puritans and Jews (aided even by Heine's comments) that Puritanism and Judaism also correspond in terms of content (Sombart 1911: 292-295). To Weber's mind, the breaking point is the presence of a dualistic economic ethic in Judaism. This means that Jews would apply other standards with respect to non-Jews than the ones used among themselves. According to Weber it is impossible to base rational economic activity on a double set of standards whereby the behaviour with the insider differs from that with the outsider (Weber 1960: 343).

Practically, however, this all-pervasive ethical dualism meant that the specific puritan idea of "proving" one's self religiously through "inner-worldly asceticism" was unavailable. For this idea could not rest on a basis which was as such objectionable, but "permissible" toward certain classes of people. Thus the religious conception of "vocational" life of ascetic Protestantism was absent from the outset. The exceptionally high (traditionalistic) esteem for religiously pursuing one's daily work... could not alter this (Weber 1960: 343-344).

Weber essentially broaches two subjects here. The first concerns the so-called dualistic ethic of Judaism and the second the place of work ethos in Judaism. Weber makes a link between them by posing that when there is a dualistic ethic, there cannot exist a work ethology comparable to that of Puritanism. We will deal with both subjects.

If, however, we first follow Weber's line of thinking and regard both subjects as interconnected, we can ask ourselves if it is indeed true that a dualistic set of standards makes proving oneself in the religious sense impossible in the economic sphere. This question is then independent of whether or not Judaism has double standards and, in our case, if there is any evidence that these ever existed among Dutch Jews.

We believe that Weber has made an essential error. When one can speak of a dualistic ethic inside one group, it is conceivable that one norm will deplete the other of its worth. When, however, one can speak of a norms system, whereby the relationship to the outsiders of that group is organized in another way than that to the insiders, there need not be negative consequences. The important point is that the insider observe the rules of both. This is possible because - although it concerns opposite standards - they organize relationships which never concur. A norms conflict is therefore made impossible. Consequently, a Jew can live up to his religious standards by scrupulously observing the economic ethic of Judaism. The essence of innerworldly asceticism is, that each action - and more precisely the "worldly" action - possesses sense and meaning. If it concerned contrary standards, this sense and meaning would come to nought. There can only be an anti-thesis when the standards govern the same case. Beyond this, the only important fact is that the ethical system be observed when acting inside and outside the group. Whether this action assumes a different form inside or outside then becomes less important.

Just what exactly is this so-called dualistic ethic? It primarily concerns the Jewish prohibition to receive interest from other Jews, while it is permitted to loan non-Jews money against interest. This is not the only matter expressing the dualistic ethic, but both Sombart and Weber regard it as the major issue.

> For our purpose, it is sufficient to state that the pious person found enough reason in the Scriptures to allow him to charge interest in business traffic with the *goyim* (Gentiles - L.D.M.): throughout the Middle Ages he was liberated from the hideous pressure of the interest-question to which Cristians were exposed. As far as I know, these privileges were never seriously questioned by the Rabbis (Sombart 1911: 286).

This passage shows the basic difference between Sombart and Weber. Both note the double ethic, but they present different interpretations. Weber says that it makes modern capitalism an impossibility, whereas Sombart considers it to promote capitalism (Sombart 1911: 292). Weber sees a modern capitalism based on rational business transactions and according to him these are impossible in a dualistic system (Weber 1965: 250).

We will first explore if this so-called double ethic was in fact so characteristic of the Jews. From Sombart as well as Weber, one is left with the impression that charging interest (immediately afterwards referred to as usury) was characteristic of the Jews. But, what was the situation in money-lending among non-Jews? Hoffman went into this at length and he comes to the conclusion that usury often assumed more serious proportions among non-Jews than Jews.

> There is, for instance, the example of Lindau, where the usurers took up to 216%, with the result that the citizens greeted the coming of the Jews with relief (Hoffmann 1910: 29).

> Innocent III wrote to the Bishof of Arras: If one followed the decrees of the Lateran Council and excluded the usurers from the church, one might as well close the churches, since there are so many of them (Hoffmann 1910: 27).

In the Middle Ages, clerical as well as worldly writers sharply condemn the usury of non-Jews who, unlike Jews, are not forced to make their living by charging interest. We note that in 1146, Bernard of Clairvaux, at the time of the second Crusade, considers that Jews should no longer be persecuted, "for the Christian usurers are even worse" (Hoffmann 1910: 26)[8].

After surveying this matter of charging interest among Jews and non-Jews, an entirely different question arises. Were Jews indeed forbidden to take interest from each other? When we consider this question, the entire matter of the double ethic appears to lack a solid foundation. It was in those very days that the Rabbis decided that Jews could take interest from each other too, because of the difficult material circumstances (Hoffmann 1910: 78). The prohibition was not lifted, but practical means were created to get around it. Palache points out, furthermore, that the Jewish Law Book - the Shulchan 'Aruch - sets out in clear terms that the non-Jew who observes the "seven laws" (in practice this refers to the Christian) must receive the same treatment as the Jew.[9] So we can speak here of a complete denial of the double ethic with respect to the Christians (Palache 1954: 193). Dünner states it with even greater clarity:

> After all, what is the lofty ideal of our prophets? Next to piety, equality, peace and reconciliation among Man. ... The Jewish people, who live in the conviction that all our non-Jewish fellow-creatures are the same as the most excellent and noblest Isrealite, as long as they recognize the Oneness of G-d and conduct a strict moral life... (Dünner 1902: 97)[10]

The problem of the dualistic ethic is more complicated, however, than would appear from the above. We have tried to show that if the point at issue had been a double ethic, it definitely concerned clearly institutionalized norms. Thereby Jewish practice - certainly in the Holland of those times - leans towards similar standards for insiders and outsiders. Weber, however, is convinced of the contrary.

> In any case, there was no soteriological motive whatever for ethically rationalizing out-group economic relations. No religious premium existed for it. That had far-reaching consequences for the economic behavior of Jews (Weber 1960: 345). However, for the Jews the realm of economic relations with strangers, particularly economic relations prohibited in regard to fellow Jews, was an area of ethical indifference (Weber 1965: 251).

Weber not only considers there to be different standards for insiders and outsiders. He goes on to suggest that beyond a double ethic there is a lack of ethics.

> The pious Jews never gauged his inner ethical standards by what he regarded as permissible in the economic context (Weber 1965: 253).

If this were the case, then one may ask if there exists extensive literature in response to this area of economic action. If the orthodox Jew didn't care if his economic behaviour was ethically correct, he would not feel the need to question the Rabbis about it (Hoffmann presents a selection from the response literature and no less than 246 responsa concerning the money trade in the Middle Ages, 1910: 124-236).

Weber also says (1960: 345) that economic success could never be evidence of the fact that a Jew had ethically proven himself in his economic behaviour, but was a consequence of his behaviour in non-economic matters. We feel this to be too definite a statement and that prosperity in general is often also seen by Jews as the possible consequence of right behaviour, including economic behaviour. Deuteronomy 25: 13-15 gives a hint in this direction, when we read that it is forbidden to use divers measures (economic behaviour) and it is promised that if this law is followed a person's days will be lengthened. Beyond that, there is such strong emphasis on an honest way of life - essentially the major point to both Weber and Sombart - throughout the Jewish literature, that we feel we ought to blame Weber's interpretations on a lack of good sources and the entire mood which has always, especially in Germany, surrounded Jews and Judaism. Weber too, has not managed to disassociate himself from this. That is why we believe the sources themselves to be the most eloquent, as follows:

> Makkoth 24a: "To speak the truth that is in his heart" (Psalm XV, 2), as R. Saphra did once. - (Rab Saphra... had a gem he wanted to sell. Someone came to see him just as he was reading Shema and cried that he was prepared to pay a certain sum of money for it, though, when he didn't receive a reply, started to offer more and more since he believed the Rabbi to be dissatisfied with the offer and therefore refused to reply. When Rab Saphra had finished, he said to the man: "You can have the gem for the amount you mentioned first. I gave you no answer, because I was reading the Shema. Inside myself, I accepted your first offer. I may not take more from you). (Tal 1881: 99-100).
> Taänit 23a: Abba Chilkya was Choni Hamaägal's grandson.

There was a drought and there were prayers for rain to be said, the scholars sent for him to pronounce the prayer. (For they, who are strictly moral and honest are the most excellent people, and most beloved by G-d). His prayer was heard every time. Once, when there was a drought, the scholars went to see him to ask him to pray for rain. They did not find him at home and went to the field where he was weeding. They greeted him, but he didn't turn to look at them. They waited until evening, when he would return home... (The scholars said: - L.D.M.) would you please explain something at which we marvelled. Why did you not turn your head when we greeted you? - "Because," replied Abba Chilkya, "today I had been hired to work for someone else, and I could not allow myself to waste a moment of another's time" (Tal 1881: 97-98).

These Talmudic quotes do not, to our mind, leave much to be desired. They indicate what the Jewish ethic is in economic acting and are far more eloquent than any precept could be. But to other minds the source alone may not be sufficiently eloquent. It is also of importance how the source was interpreted in later years. To demonstrate this, here are some quotes from the sermons of Chief Rabbi Dünner, held in Amsterdam:

The only duties G-d gives us are to lead an upright and honest life, to practice charity, to see that brides in distress are given in marriage and to give the poor an honourable burial (Dünner 1902: 81).

and

Whoever does not observe honesty and sincerity in his behaviour towards his neighbour... loses the right to call himself an Israelite (Dünner 1902: 81).

This opinion about the Jewish ethic did not only come from the pulpit orators: other people who were in actual contact with Jews were positive in their comments as well. We refer you to the passage in Dubnow (1927: 426) quoted earlier. It is also known that the Kings of the House of Orange, who often had business dealings with Jews, praised their honesty (Tal 1898: 60). Even in Justus van Effen's *Hollandsche Spectator* we find a comment about the Jews:

that he had frequently found more honesty among them than among Christians (S.K. 1925: 54).

Weber nevertheless reaches the conclusion that there is no evidence anywhere of an appreciation of economic activity as a virtue (Weber 1960: 254). We ask ourselves if it is conceivable that when the "right" way of life plays such an important role and we see that the scholars themselves are involved economically, one can reasonably assume that the economic activity itself is not part of the ethical system and is not seen as a virtue.

Contrary to what Weber says, there are very clear indications which makes one suspect the opposite. For instance, it is a father's duty to teach his son a "light and clean trade" (Tal 1930: 22). In addition there are Talmudic quotes, which prove the opposite:

> Berachot 8a: Noble is the man who fears G-d, but still better the man who thereby enjoys the labour of his hands (Tal 1930: 43).
> Shabbath 63a: It is much better to lend the needy person a sum of money than to give it to him. But what deserves the most merit is to give him goods for sale and then let him enjoy half of the profit (Tal 1881: 40).

This last act not only gets him out of his financial difficulties, but also back into economic life.

The error made by both Weber and Sombart, consists of them not having made a difference between morality and law. From the non-Jewish side one constantly attempts to characterise the Jewish ethic on the basis of legal standards. This doesn't explain much, since Jewish law is concerned with defining territories and therefore arrives at strict and undifferentiated pronouncements. These must, however, be understood and executed in the spirit of the moral law. So when a case is being dealt with in which is being determined how much "zuz" is owed the one party and how much the other and there are lengthy debates to reach an extremely accurate verdict, then this does not alter the fact that a few sentences further along one is advised to give "more than the measure of law". And this concept is the true ethical orientation of the Jew (Tal 1881: 102-103).

From this, all Weber's and Sombart's problems regarding double standards and about honesty in general, can be understood. Basically, it is possible to find everything in Talmudic literature, even quite opposite pronouncements. The determining factor, however, is the ethical frame of reference. Even an investigation of sources does not suffice here. It is the manner of application and execution that counts, also in view of the fact that a Jew, generally, has learnt to be honest to Jew and non-Jew from infancy. This does not exclude that there have been exceptions. These were mostly a consequence of circumstances, however, which the non-Jewish population forced on the Jewish one and which made life unbearable.[11]

The above might easily leave the impression that we agree with Sombart's ideas and criticism of Weber.

> ...yes: so that what we call Puritanism is not really, when we look at its characteristic features, Judaism (Sombart 1911: 226).

But this is not the case: we believe that there are countless differences to be listed between Puritanism and Judaism - even if we restricted ourselves to the entirely different structure of the life of a Jew, in which the legal aspect plays such an important part, or to the doctrine of election of the Puritan - which make this identification impossible. Neither Sombart nor Weber have thereby differentiated between the various trends in Judaism. The innerworldly asceticism for instance, does in principle exist in Judaism.[12] However, the differences on this point between various groups of Jews are so vast that one cannot pose that Jews everywhere live a typically ascetic life, although the religious laws refer to an ascetic philosophy of life. Among the Portuguese Jews, whom we have taken as an example of a group with a modern capitalistic attitude, there was little evidence of this asceticism. The data tend to point the other way. We find a reference to some 24 country houses along the river Vecht (Zwarts 1922: 6; Da Silva Rosa 1925: 82). The stage and music represent favourite pastimes and there are even chambers of rhetoric (Da Silva Rosa 1925: 103). From the descriptions of travellers who visited Amsterdam we learn of the great luxury exhibited by the Portuguese Jews, which often surpassed that of European rulers (Da Silva Rosa 1925: 113). So one could hardly say that the Portuguese Jews were ascetic.[13]

We hope, with this description of Judaism and a closer look at the Portuguese Jews, to have demonstrated that Weber made a wrong assessment of the content of Judaism. Secondly that the thesis that the modern capitalistic mentality could not be found back in Judaism is untenable and thirdly that modern capitalism does not have to be linked to innerwordly asceticism. After we have seen how this last link has worked in other religions, we will try to show to what Judaism owes the modern capitalistic mentality.

Capitalism and ethic in India and China 3.

Weber's work about India and China can be seen as proof for his thesis concerning the connection between the spirit of modern capitalism and the Protestant ethic. After all, he keeps trying to show that the economic structure is linked to the ethical teachings of the group in question and that the connection he speaks of cannot be found because of the other ethic. We will present a brief sketch here of the religions of India and China in so far this has a bearing on what we want to show, i.e. that it is possible to make other connections between ethics and economic structure than were observed by Weber.

3.1 *Hinduism*

In view of the above, we will not go deeply into the contentual side of Hindu ethics. The form, which is determined by the caste system, is of greater importance, since each caste (jati) and class (varna) distinguishes itself from the other by its own norms. So there is no universal ethic, and every status and professional group distinguishes itself by having its own "dharma" (Weber 1967: 172). One facet of these ethics is that a person engages in the specific profession of the caste, which is again associated with specific standards.

So a member of the warrior class gains nothing, at least ethically, by observing the standards of the other class. His ethics require him to wage war and not, like the Brahman, to perform ritual services. Nor can one pose that in this way he lives the most meaningful life - although it is as meaningful as is possible within his class. The class system represents a continuous confrontation between different ways of life, of which some are more meaningful than others and which are not accessible to everyone.

In orthodox Hinduism there still exists the difference between layman and monk and other renouncers of the world (sannyasin). This means that there are different roads towards salvation, whereby the monk can reach the highest form of personal holiness. The layman can reach a better incarnation by leading an ethical life. In a next life he can be born into a higher class. Layman and monk do not only go separate roads, but have separate goals as well. The achievement of the layman cannot therefore be compared to that of the monk (Weber 1967: 174).

Hinduism, next to separate ways of living, also presents one with a large gap between the great mass of the people and the religious elite. Brahmanic teachings are relatively meaningless to the majority of Hindus. Sometimes laymen are not even familiar with the names of Shiva and Vishnu (Weber 1967: 327). In addition, Hinduism assumes several forms which appreciably differ from one another in practice.

As to the form of the asceticism, we can simplify the many things we might say about it by establishing that Hindu asceticism is not innerworldly, like it is in Puritanism, but otherworldly (Weber 1967: 337-338).

The highest caste of the Brahmans also constitutes an elite group in the economic sphere. Weber quotes figures which indicate that the higher castes, including the Brahmans, have a relatively high position on the social scale, at least when incomes are measured (Weber 1967: 116). The Brahmans were occupying special positions long before the Middle Ages. They acquired property in exchange for the ritual services they performed for the aristocracy (Weber 1967: 321). From this, however, not a trace of modern capitalism developed. The Indian factory worker displays the typical traits of what Weber means by traditional capitalism: He wants to get rich as quickly as possible and work as little as possible. Higher earnings do not inspire greater achievements but lead to taking more time off. If someone wishes to stay away from work he does so. Discipline in the European sense is an unknown concept (Weber 1967: 114).[14] Where a traditional trade was practised, people often managed to acquire some possessions. However, industrialisation in the modern sense of the word was impossible on the basis of the caste system.

> ..., it must still be considered extremely unlikely that the modern organization of industrial capitalism would ever have originated on the basis of the caste system. A ritual law in which every change of occupation, every change in work technique may result in ritual degradation is certainly not capable of giving birth to economic and technical revolutions from within itself, or even of facilitating the first germination of capitalism in its midst (Weber 1967: 112).

The last is not contradicted by the practical possibilities for industry in relation to the caste system. The basic problem of the caste structure was that members of clean and unclean castes could not touch each other and were therefore unable to work together. Where the working space of the tradesman was concerned - and therefore the factory - these rules were not applied in quite so stringent a manner. However, the entire atmosphere of the caste system rebels, as Weber remarks, against every form of co-operation between the castes (Weber 1967: 112).

So Hinduism distinguishes itself in many fashions from Puritanism, even apart from the contentual differences. It has an entirely different labour ethology. The concept "rastlose Berufsarbeit" (insistent call to work) that characterized the Puritans, cannot be applied here. There is a separate order of priests to perform ritual services. Each status group has its own ethics and in addition there are vast differences between the elite and the mass of the people. Furthermore, innerworldly asceticism did not play a role in Hinduism.

3.2 *Buddhism*

We can be equally brief about Buddhism in showing what is relevant to our case, i.e. we will not delve into the content of the ethical system, but confine ourselves to the form.

When we do refer to the content of the doctrine, then this serves to demonstrate how far this is removed from the rationalism of the Calvinist doctrine. Instead of standing in the world and interacting with it, the Buddhist tries to escape the world.

> For salvation from the endless struggle of eternally renewed individuality in order to achieve everlasting tranquillity could be achieved only by giving up every "thirst" linking man to the world of imperfection and the struggle for existence. Naturally, such salvation was accessible only to the "homeless" (*pabbajita,* that is to say, economy-less) status group, according to parish doctrine only the wandering disciples (who in later times were called monks, *Bhikkshu*). In the parish doctrine the status group of "house-dwelling people" ...existed only for the purpose of sustaining by alms the Buddhist disciple who aspires to the state of grace until he has reached it (Weber 1967: 214).

The last immediately brings us to the form, whereby it is striking that dualism once more plays a part: there are ethics for the layman and separate ethics for the monk.

While for the monks there are quite unambiguous moral rules, the founder limits himself as regards the pious adorers to a few advisory recommendations which were only later and gradually developed in a sort of lay ethic (Weber 1967: 215).

The principal characteristic of this lay ethic is that it is not as meaningful as the ethic of the monk. The layman is not enabled to perform the same ethical achievements which lead to salvation (Weber 1967: 215). This had its consequences for the greater mass of the people.

Precisely the absolute extra-worldly character, the cultlessness of the monkish piety, and the lack of any kind of planned influence on life conduct of the laity - a very important difference between ancient Buddhism and Jainism - must have pushed the lay piety increasingly in the direction of hagiolatry and idolatry as it was practiced by the later Mahayana sects (Weber 1967: 222).

The only means whereby the layman could essentially improve his spiritual fate was the maintenance of the monks (Weber 1967: 214). It is clear that this made the matter of providing one's own ethic with meaning extremely questionable. And Buddhism does not have a professional ethic either, whereby the profession can become the vocation, as in Puritanism. Buddhism is also basically anti-ascetic, at least when we think of asceticism as a rational way of life, as Weber does (Weber 1967: 220). Although Buddhism indicates a certain specific way to arrive at enlightenment, one may not follow its path through a rational insight into the principles on which it is metaphysically based or through gradual training in greater moral perfection. Liberation is reached through a sudden jump in the psychic state of enlightenment, which can only be gained through systematic contemplation (Weber 1967: 220). In general, there are important differences with Puritanism.

The Buddhistic monastic mores not only exclude work but also the otherwise usual ascetic means, except for auxiliary practices for deepening contemplation, edification for securing self-control through confession, and admonition of the student by the teacher, the junior disciples by senior monks. Buddhism denies any form of rational asceticism (Weber 1967: 219).

So here too we see that the form of the ethic displays differences with Puritanism as it did with Hinduism. There is a similar difference between the ethics of the elite and the greater mass of the people, i.e.

the religious order and the laity. Although Buddhism, unlike Hinduism, does not have a strictly social stratification with a separate set of standards for each caste, we can nevertheless observe great differences between the various Buddhist groups. The monasteries, at an early date, had land, buildings and slaves and the monks clearly enjoyed another status than the laity (Weber 1967: 223). Nor did innerworldly asceticism play a part.

3.3 Jainism

Jainism is of particular interest to us, because in this group we encounter a positive relationship between a religious conviction and an economic motivation which is absent in other Indian religions, i.e. Jains constitute a sect of merchants even more exclusive than Jews were in the West (Weber 1967: 193).[15]

> It may be noted that the acquisition of considerable wealth was in no way forbidden, only the striving after wealth and attachment to riches; this was rather similar to the ascetic Protestantism of the Occident. As with Protestantism, "joy in possessions" (*parigraha*) was the objectional thing, but not possession or gain in itself. The similarity extends further: a Jain commandment forbids saying anything false or exaggerated; the Jains believed in absolute honesty in business life, all deception (*maya*) was prohibited, including especially all dishonest gain through smuggling, bribery, and any sort of disreputable financial practice (*adattu dama*) (Weber 1967: 200).

They applied the same dictum as the Quakers did in the West: "honesty is the best policy". Consequently they were renowned for their honesty. They also had the reputation of being very rich. In many opinions, more than half of Indian trade passed through their hands (Weber 1967: 200). According to Weber, this wealth is not merely connected to their honest way of life, but also relates to their systematic life-style. They have to abstain from all intoxicating substances, and also from meat and honey, they have to be absolutely faithful in marriage and may not engage in immoral practices, they have to avoid pride and rage and must suppress all passions (Weber 1967: 201). They resemble the Puritans in this as well. Because of their ascetic way of life they were virtually forced to save and they could invest money, the same as the Puritans did. Because of their ritual limitations, says Weber, they were excluded from industry and stopped at trade capitalism (Weber 1967: 200).

Their asceticism assumes extreme forms. It is not the same kind as in Puritanism though.

> He achieves supreme holiness who starves himself to death. On the whole, however, this asceticism as compared to the primitive asceticism of magicians, is spiritualized in the direction of "world renunciation". "Homelessness" is the basic holy concept. It signifies the break of all worldly relations, thus, above all indifference to all sense perceptions and avoidance of all action based on worldly motives. It aims at seeking to cease to "act", to hope, and to wish (Weber 1967: 195-196).

Although the form of the asceticism is other than that in Puritanism, it nevertheless results in a very methodical way of life, as we remarked earlier. Yet one may ask to what extent the ethical system of Jainism still makes life meaningful. What is one to think of a life which requires a person to stop acting, hoping and wishing? One answer to this might be that this analysis of the content of Jain ethics has been put too simply. For how can we imagine anyone actually stopping with these three things and yet continuing ordinary family life? That is to say that the Jain, just because of this combination of laydom and asceticism will continously have to inquire into the meaning of each act (and not only each act). This produces a kind of rationality, which puts a person in a position to practice capitalism. In this case, industry does not develop either because of restricting circumstances, just as we have tried to demonstrate with Judaism. Here too, we see that capitalism - we will not define the nature of that capitalism here - is not necessarily linked to innerworldly asceticism, but to another form of asceticism.[16] One might deduct from the preceding quotation that it shouldn't be posed that life is meaningful, but that death is. In other words: to stop living is meaningful. Although this might be an ideal, practice shows us that we are concerned with a living community whose members have to consider and weigh each act within the framework of their ideal and everything therefore gains meaning.

As we saw in other Indian religions, there are laymen and monks, but the distance between them is, as we shall see, less great in Jainism.

> ... so among the Jainas the highest calling is to the order of *yatis* (strivers) while the lower calling is less demanding for the *shravakas* (hearers, referring to the laity)... Right conduct was similar in principle for *yatis* and *shravakas*, but the former pursued the rules more intensely (Baird & Bloom 1972: 44). In spite of the strict disciplinary subordination of the laity (*cravaka*)

79

under the monk-clergy, the former have always exerted strong influence in Jainism (Weber 1967: 202).

One might rightly speak of a difference in quantity here: there is not, in the first instance, a qualitative difference between laity and monastic order. The ambition of the laity closely resembles that of the monks.

The duties of the laymen did not basically differ from those of the monks: contrary to Hinduism, one knew only one holy purpose and only one form of perfection. The *dharma* of the laity consisted of trying to come as close as possible to that of the monks (Lemmen 1977: 86).

Consequently Weber calls the laity "professional monks", whereby the stress is laid more on the laity and their systems than on schools and monasteries (Weber 1967: 196). The layman was in fact required to lead a monastic life, though he could remain a layman. So the layman had to spend 48 minutes a day meditating. On special days - four times a month - he had to lead the life of a monk (Weber 1967: 198). Nor was there a separate priestly class with its personal ethics. Ritual services could be performed by the laity. Sometimes Brahmans were employed to care for the temple, but this wasn't a necessity (Baird & Bloom 1972: 47). In this aspect they once more resemble the Puritans.

Jainism leaves one with the impression that it has one ethical system. The clerical elite and the laity do not have separate standards. Although this is not an entirely accurate picture - there is, after all, a separate groups of monks - one cannot quite speak of two separate and different ethical systems. So it is not surprising that the ethics have been internalized by the greater mass of the people as well. Bouquet remarks that their moral level is extremely high: it is rare for a Jain to commit an offence (Bouquet 1967: 162).

3.4 *Religion in China*

China is typified by having an ethic for the greater mass of the people and an ethic for the elite. The religion of the first group is Taoism, whereas the second group adhered to Confucianism. This latter group ruled the Imperial State and had to prove, through exams, to have acquired enough knowledge of the classics.

Insofar as it was oriented to orthodoxy the whole imperial administration was controlled by an essentially theocratic board of literati (Weber 1964: 102).

The Confucian therefore invested his capital in the first instance in building up a career. And not only personal capital was used for an education in classic literature; the entire family assisted, which meant, later on, that the successful candidate let his clan share in his status. There was a trace of rationality in this as well. But not the same rationality as was found in Puritanism which provided the impulse to control the world, though a rationalism which meant adjustment to the world (Weber 1964: 247-248).

The Chinese did not deliberately cut himself off from the impressions and influence of the "world" - a world which the Puritan sought to control, just as he did himself, by means of a definite and one-sided rational effort of will. The Puritan was taught to suppress the petty acquisitiveness which destroys all rational, methodical enterprise - an acquisitiveness which distinguishes the conduct of the Chinese shopkeeper (Weber 1964: 244).

Wealth did not proceed from rational profit-making (Weber 1964: 86). Insofar as wealth played a part in the life of the Confucian, it played a different part than in Puritanism, although it was highly important indeed. Wealth was considered the most perfect means to arrive at a virtuous, i.e. a dignified, way of life. Improving mankind was therefore read as enriching mankind, for only a rich man could meet the obligations of position and status (Weber 1964: 245). So this resulted in a money-hungry attitude without there being the kind of rationality that characterizes modern capitalistic enterprise.

The Chinese shopkeeper haggled for and reckoned with every penny and he daily counted over his cash receipts. Reliable travellers reported that the conversation of the native Chinese was about money and money affairs, apparently to an extant seldom found elsewhere. But it is very striking that out of this unceasing and intensive economic ado and the much bewailed crass "materialism" of the Chinese, there failed to originate on the economic plane those great and methodical business conceptions which are rational in nature and are presupposed by modern capitalism (Weber 1964: 242).

This irrational element also manifested itself in the distrust of the Confucian gentlemen. He distrusted everyone else, and he similarly assumed others to distrust him. The dictum "honesty is the best policy" that featured so much in Puritanism as well as in Jainism, formed no part of his philosophy. This fundamental distrust interfered with all economic transactions, especially where credit systems were concerned (Weber 1964: 232, 244). The rationalism required for capitalism was missing (Weber 1964: 100-104). The great wealth of the mandarins who had retired from imperial service was not invested in commercial ventures but in land (Weber 1964: 85). There is also no evidence that there were ever any large-scale ventures in capitalistic factory systems (Weber 1964: 97). It is interesting to note, however, that it was the Mandarin group who put money into capitalistic enterprises when China was under Western influence. When the Chinese railways were built for example (Weber 1964: 199, 244). This would only seem natural because they were financially in the best position. It is significant that they - once the opportunity arose - stopped putting their money into land, but were sensitive to capitalistic ways of making profits. Unless this is regarded as just another form of speculation, they cannot be denied a rationalism belonging to capitalistic behaviour.

The ethic of Confucianism can be realized only by the elite, so its meaning is of little practical use where the greater mass of the people are concerned (Weber 1964: 230).

> The Confucian desired "salvation" only from the barbaric lack of education. As the reward of virtue he expected only long life, health and wealth in this world and beyond death the retention of his good name (Weber 1964: 228).

The Confucian ideals are typically elite ideals, which can be realized exclusively by a small group of people, especially where a non-modern society is concerned. Other differences between elite and the masses could be found in the sceptical attitude of the Confucian towards magic, which was of extreme importance to the Taoist common faith. Weber speaks of "the magic garden of heterodox doctrine" when he mentions Taoism (Weber 1964: 227).

> Above all - and this is especially important for us - they were also differentiated socially - on the one side (and in small part) indeed in terms of the stratum to which they were native; on the other side, however, (and primarily) in terms of the form of hope they offered different strata of their adherents. The first phenomenon was partly expressed in such a manner that the upper social strata stood against the folk soteriology of the masses, abruptly denying all salvation religiosity. China presented this type. It was partly the case that different social strata cherished different forms of soteriology. ... The same religions dispensed different forms of holy values and in terms of these

made demands of variable strength on the different social strata (Weber 1967: 330).

The above very clearly reveals the point we want to emphasize: in Indian and Chinese religions there is always a division into an elite religion and a popular belief. They are both associated with different classes in society. This is an important difference with Puritanism and Judaism, and also Jainism.

Confucianism does not include asceticism either.

Conclusion 4.

After having examined the relationship between ethics and capitalism in a number of religions, we now want to compare, as Sombart and Weber did, several facets of Judaism and Puritanism to arrive at a conclusion about the connection between ethics and capitalism. We will also investigate what the specific differences between these two religions and the other religions and ethical systems we have discussed are. We will thereby confine ourselves to the main points.

The outstanding point in Judaism and Puritanism is the form of the ethical system. In both cases one can speak of a *singular ethical system* in contrast with Chinese and Indian religions, which have a *dualistic ethical system* and separate standards for the elite and the masses. To speak of two ethical systems would not be sufficient: in all cases it concerns groups who together represent largely a single group. These groups are stratified, however, into elite and masses. Jainism is an exception to the rule.

In Puritanism this is strongly expressed through the lack of a separate clerical order. In some Protestant sects this emphasis on the laity has continued to exist, whereas in others the minister is a separate functionary. Nowhere in Protestantism can one speak, however, of a religious order. The same applies to Judaism.

> The rabbis were no exclusively secular and above all no status group of genteel jurists like the Roman jurisconsuls, but plebeian teachers of religious ritual (Weber 1960: 414).

Although Judaism has had an order resembling a monastic community, like that of the Essenes for instance, this should be seen as a departure from the rule. The whole monastic idea and the accompanying rejection of the world is generally foreign to Judaism.

> The concept of monasticism and hermitage asceticism is entirely foreign to the Talmud. Talmud scholars and rabbis consider it contrary to human duty to take one's leave of the world, society

and all earthly joys. They do not consider the world to be purely a "valley of tears" (Tal 1881: 33).

Through this co-ordination of laity and clergy, Puritanism differed considerably from Roman Catholicism:
> Although the rules of life of the Catholic monastic orders are on the whole governed by similar aims and exercises, Puritan asceticism in one aspect essentially differs from that of the monks: it is demanded from all the faithful and has to be practised in "the world", whereas the monk, as a member of a religious elite escapes "the world" because of his ascetic ideal (Tennekes 1969: 367).

Puritanism and Judaism - at the present we have tried to make this claim only in the case of the Portuguese Jews - share another important element. In both instances the ethical system appears to be very well internalized. The Portuguese Jews were reputed to be particularly honest merchants - as was mentioned earlier. In Calvinism ethical behaviour was registered as if book were being kept in which daily life represented a business enterprise (Weber 1958: 124).

In Judaism too there exists a "drawing up of the balance". In some movements there was and is a strong emphasis on this. The special reason for this is that ethical behaviour can also be expressed in following a great number of formal rules which makes it possible to check if they have been observed. This ethical awareness characterizes the Protestant as well. Kruijt has paid attention to the differences in attitude of the various sections of the population in The Netherlands. He quotes a number of passages which reveal that there are differences between the Roman Catholic and the Calvinist:
> (quotes van der Leeuw:) The Roman Catholic believes... he can leave all kinds of things to look after themselves; he has dogma and clergy. The Protestant cannot let others decide, not even the minister; frequently he is obstinate and conceited, but he is aware of his own responsibility. (The Roman Catholic is characterized by - L.D.M.)... unconcern which can lead to flightiness and which strongly contrasts with the strict attitude to life and the pessimism of the Calvinist part of the population... (quotes Antoon Coolen about the mentality of the Roman Catholic:) His joviality has the drawback that he is lax.

and
> With the acceptance of the faith, the Limburger considers he has

looked after the principal matter. The rest will be taken care of by the Lord and the Saints (Kruijt 1968: 32-33).

The Catholic will let himself more easily be tempted in the matter of small shortcomings, as Kruijt suggests. The Protestant frowns on even the smallest shortcoming (Kruijt 1968: 37-38).[17]

It is striking that in Judaism as well as in Puritanism the variable, which corresponds, is the singular nature of the ethical system. For although there is a liberal measure of innerworldly asceticism being practised in Judaism, we were not able to find this among the Portuguese Jews. Also, Judaism and Puritanism share this factor with Jainism, which we stated had a very well internalized norms system. After all, the Jains are known for the small incidence of crime among them. We would therefore like to conclude from this that the form which the ethical system assumes - either a singular ethical system, or a dualistic ethical system - is an important factor in promoting a modern capitalism. In the three religions we have mentioned we find a special capitalistic development, which does not occur elsewhere.[18] We keep finding a well internalized ethic, whereby meaningful action is made possible. It makes the action methodical and rational, which is the foundation for a modern capitalistic development. We are not forgetting that the content of the ethical system is of paramount importance. But this content can only be used in a meaningful way when its form is singular.[19] Only this can safeguard the individual from confusion when he keeps being confronted with an elite system, which is more meaningful than his own system, as is the case with Indian and Chinese religions. Not just the masses are the victims under two systems. Dualism has its consequences for the elite as well. A capitalistic development - especially industry - becomes far less likely because it requires the co-operation of the entire group. Even when the elite has sufficient means at its disposal, a modern capitalism cannot get started because the masses are unfit to perform the work required.

In Tennekes' study about the "Old Dutch-Reformed" these differences in the form of the ethical system are examined as well. He compares two Protestant groups in present-day Holland, i.e. the Dutch Reformed and the Old Dutch-Reformed. Among the latter it is possible to make a distinction between converts and the non-converted:

> The internal structure of the Dutch Reformed church communities ... varies drastically. There is no question of a division within the community into convert and non-convert. And the

community as a whole is addressed by the minister as "congregation of the Lord" and in principle all the adult members partake of the Lord's Supper (Tennekes 1969: 377-378). This is not the case among the "Old Dutch-Reformed": A typical illustration of their ambiguous position is their attitude towards the Lord's Supper, "which the Lord has ordained for only the faithful" (i.e. the "converts"). Although anyone who was confirmed can formally partake of the Lord's Supper, no one who knows he is not converted will do so. It is one of the few examples of a clear institutionalisation of the fundamental division in the congregation (Tennekes 1969: 376).

With the Old Dutch-Reformed, Tennekes speaks in terms of elite and followers, whereby the converts, who assume the role of leaders, constitute the elite (Tennekes 1969: 376-377). There are also differences between the Dutch Reformed and Old Dutch-Reformed in economic and social activism. The first are cognizant of a cultural mission. The aspiration to succeed is religiously justified, whereas the latter lack this particular ambition (Tennekes 1969: 380). This is rather strange because from the article in question it appears that innerworldly asceticism very much exists among the Old Dutch-Reformed (Tennekes 1969: 378). Tennekes believes this to be due to the way in which the question of election by the Old Dutch-Reformed has been formulated:

The central point of the "Old Dutch-Reformed" understanding of faith is the question "am I elected" - which is not the case with the Dutch-Reformed. If the latter are asked this question, it has a paralysing rather than an activating effect. However, since this question is not generally asked in quite such a way by the "Dutch Reformed", they distinguish themselves from the "Old Dutch-Reformed" by a greater economic and social activism (Tennekes 1969: 383-384).

We would like to go into greater detail concerning this conclusion. The election question does not, by itself, have to lead to inactivism. In this case, however, the consequence of asking the question is that society has been split into two groups of people whose ethics differ. This does not mean that each one has separate ethics, but that they practise them in a divergent manner. This leads to a division whereby only the elite is able to conduct a meaningful life and because of this, depletes the system of meaning of the followers. In other words: if the question had not led to division, the consequences would probably have been different.[20]

In conclusion there are some general comments to be made, based on the above. When there is a want of a universal ethic, as is always the case in Catholic countries, the basis for healthy capitalism is missing. There will always exist a difference between the formal elitist belief and the popular religion. This makes internalisation of the "church" norms impossible and causes them to be enforced from the top. From this, one can deduct that Catholic countries are more sensitive to totalitarian regimes than Protestant countries. Another possibility is the total secularisation of society, so that another ethic can be introduced. We might expect a development of this kind in all countries with dualistic ethical systems. If the church or the established authorities keep control of the ethic and the power, one can expect a right-wing government. If there is a secularisation process first, then the social thinking of a left-wing government will have more appeal. However, in both cases it will require a totalitarian regime to force the population to accept either the new or the old norms. In South East Asia, where ethical dualism is constantly present, we might therefore expect a development of this nature. As far as the Catholic countries are concerned, the only way to oppose communism and a totalitarian regime might well be the promotion of further equalization between laity and clergy, a development which has already made considerable progress.

Notes

1. This article would not have been realised in this version without the critical observations of a great number of readers. I am practicably grateful to Drs. J. J. Groenemeijer, Drs. A. Rienks, Dr. J. M. Schoffeleers, Prof. Dr. J. Schoorl, Prof. Dr. J. Tennekes, Drs. G. van Tillo and Drs. A. D. Willemier Westra. Of course they are not in any way responsible for the contents and the conclusions that were drawn.

   I would also like to thank the Free University for the subsidy which made it possible to have this paper translated into English and Mrs. G. Kilburn for the way she performed this task.

1a. In orthodox Jewish practice the word describing the Almighty is never written in full and, in quoting, I have followed this practice in this paper.

2. Rationalization therefore implies that the process of meaningful interpretation, since it is based on a criterium of some kind, has a conscious, and in consequence, a systematic character (Lemmen 1977: 101).

3. ... we can summarize Weber's main contention by saying that modern capitalism, as against other historical types, is characterized by its formal rationality. 'Formal' rationality involves an assessment of the extent to which actions are calculated in terms of opportunities, needs and relative costs and are thus directly related to goals that are empirically quantifiable. This contrasts with 'substantive' rationality... which refers rather to questions of ultimate ends: 'salvation' would be just an ultimate end, as would 'the greatest happiness of the greatest number'. Ultimate ends are not capable of being empirically calculated and quantified in the way that 'discrete' ends are, though they may nevertheless influence action (Hill 1973: 125-126).

   When, in future, we speak of rationality, we mean formal rationality.

4. An important part of this discussion has already taken place in the past. Sombart's anti-semitic book drew many reactions from the Jewish world. A striking example of this is Dr. M. Hoffmann's "Judentum und Kapitalismus".

5. De Quiros' book is being quoted here because of its interesting details. It is not known, however, which sources supplied the writer with information.

6. Menasshe ben Israel's concern was other than might have been supposed, i.e. he was of the opinion that it would be necessary for the coming of the Messiah that the Jews be scattered throughout the corners of the earth. There were no Jews in England at that time. So it was necessary for Jews to establish themselves there as well. It probably didn't matter to him whether they were Dutch or Spanish Jews (Da Silva Rosa 1925: 50).

7. Luther even makes recommendations to raze all synagogues with the ground, to destroy Jewish houses, take away their religious books and make work impossible for them (Dubnow 1927: 203). The other Reformers were generally less anti-semitic, although one can hardly speak of positive influences on their part.

8. One may wonder what bearing the charging of interest by Jews and Christians in the Middle Ages has on our subject. After all, we are concentrating on the time of the Reformation. Weber's as well as Sombart's thinking about double standards is based on an existing course of events which had its roots in an earlier period and from which the view was born that the Jews were pre-eminently usurers. Aside from that, it is very much in question if at a later date too, the Jews can be given the monopoly of double standards. During a courtcase in Holland in 1690, in which a foreigner from Konigsberg was involved who had cheated a number of

Jews in a business transaction, the deceiver commented that he believed that "here, as in his own country, it was permitted to deceive Jews" (Baalde 1935: 113).

9. These seven laws are: the appointment of judges and the commandments not to blaspheme, to practise idolatry, to commit murder, to commit incest, to steal and to eat meat taken from a living animal (Palache 1954: 191).

10. The quotes make it evident, that certainly in the case of The Netherlands and in our dissertation about Portuguese Jews we are dealing with The Netherlands - non-Jews were regarded as not differing from Jews. That these statements in part originate from Ashkenazi Rabbis does not alter this fact, since it is quite correct to pose that the Dutch Jews constituted a unity where matters of this nature were concerned. Nor does it preclude the existence of different views in other countries. We believe, however, that it is essential, even when there exist different norms for insider and outsider, that these norms be clearly defined and both sets of standards be observed. Weber doubts if the latter is put into practice: "What is prohibited in relation to one's brothers is permitted in relation to strangers" (Weber 1965: 250). This is too easy a statement.

11. The people who have investigated the so-called double standards have never troubled to find positive elements in them. These exist, nevertheless. In what is called the Sabbatical Year, all debts, for instance, owing from one Jew to another, lapse. Debts to non-Jews must be paid however. Also in cases where a Jew has been the guarantor to a non-Jew for another Jew, the guarantor must see to it that the debt is paid, whereas normally all debts among Jews themselves are declared to have expired. This facet of "double standards" is usually suppressed (Kitsur Shulchan 'Aruch 180: 12). Then there is the fact that every double standard is made impossible where non-Jews themselves apply standards according to the norm that the state law must be considered Jewish law. This applies to civil law (Kitsur Shulchan 'Aruch 182: 16).

12. Among the Chassidim, asceticism is sometimes one of the principal traits in serving G-d (Meijers 1974: 121-127).

13. The most radical forms of the rationalized persuasion ethic completely reject art as being in direct conflict with religious purpose. Innerworldly asceticism sees art as a flight into irrational spheres at the cost of rational labour in the world (Lemmen 1977: 119-120).

14. There has been some change in the situation since Weber's time. Drs. C. J. G. van der Burg of the Institute of Religious Studies of the Free University, for whose remarks about the section on Indian religions I am very grateful, informed me that nowadays the purport of my article largely applied only to the civil servant class and that there is generally little evidence of a work ethos that provides the daily task with meaning.

15. The word "sect" here is Weber's.

16. It might be possible to show that the nature of capitalism in Jainism is also more modern than Weber suggests. We will leave this opinion for what it is, since we do not have the right sources at our disposal. It is plain, however, that the rational element that upholds capitalism is partly present. Weber's comments about the magic nature of Jainism do not detract from this. It still remains to be seen if every form of magic ought to be considered irrational. Most especially where the view, that magic is a primitive form of technology, is concerned and where one might consider magic a rational proces.

17. Bonger records that there is more criminality among Catholics in Holland, in a period when there was still a clear distinction between laity and clergy, than among Protestants and Jews (1917: 10-11), but arrives at the conclusion that the high incidence of criminality among Catholice is linked to their social circumstances, which includes poverty (1917: 26, 28). It is not recognized that poverty, as well as deviation from the norms, can be a consequence of a double ethical system, although one must not look upon the position of the Dutch Catholics out of the context of a number of restricting historical circumstances. This problem has not passed unnoticed in Catholic circles and has resulted in the most singular statements, including an emphasis on racial aptitude and the withdrawal of intellect from the Catholic part of the nation through the celibacy of the clergy (Feber 1940: 100). We cannot seriously accept such statements. Besides, Bonger also says - even though he does not provide detailed background information - that the figures for criminality for Catholics in Switzerland equal those of other persuasions (Bonger 1917: 32).

18. The rise of capitalism in Japan has been left out of this discussion. There too, the same rule applies, i.e. that modern capitalism does not occur in Japan until after the Restoration, after Shinto has been introduced as state religion and the influence of other religions is discouraged. By doing so, Japan had a singular ethical system which made it possible to act rationally.

19. Meaningful action cannot simply be defined as formal rational action. Meaningful behaviour is its first prerequisite however. The action must be based on norms and these norms need to be well internalized. Our emphasis on good internalization of the norms system is of immediate importance to the possibility of rational action. Earlier on, we quoted Hill who discusses formal rationality in terms of calculation. Or as Lemmen says: "It is a question of action in relation to aims, means and secondary consequences. One consciously weighs means against ends or one verifies which secondary consequences will result from certain purposes or what the possible alternatives might be" (1977: 49). For a calculation of this nature it is necessary to know what might be expected from the other person in a certain situation. In other words: there need to exist specific norms for every action and these need to be observed. This presupposes a great deal of internalization, which can only be expected from a singular ethical system.

20. This is ample proof, we hope, that our independent variable is not the stratification of the group, i.e. its being characterized by one or more status groups, but the form of the ethical system. In the case of the Old Dutch-Reformed, the content of the ethic leads to a division into two different status groups and not vice versa. It is also highly unlikely that the Portuguese Jews for instance, who operated from a singular ethical system, had no stratification in their community. However, this was not similar to Catholicism, for instance, where different ethical systems led to a distinction between laity and clergy.

    The content of the ethical system determines the form. If certain doctrines tend to produce a dualistic ethical system, then it is only natural that the various systems will have different status groups, although logically a reverse order must not be excluded.

    The critical factor, however, which makes a system of meaning effective, is its singular or dualistic nature: otherwise stated, the form, independent of its cause.

Bibliography

Baelde, R.
    1935 Studiën over godsdienstdelicten. (Studies about religious offences.) The Hague.

Baird, Robert D. & Bloom, Alfred.
    1972 Indian and Far Eastern Religious Traditions. New York, Evanston, San Francisco, London.

Bendix, Reinhard.
    1962 Max Weber, an intellectual portrait. Garden City, New York.

Bonger, W. A.
    1917 Geloof en misdaad. (Faith & Crime.) Amsterdam, Rotterdam.

Bouquet, A. C.
    1967 Grote religies. Vergelijking en waardering. (Comparative religion.) Utrecht, Antwerp.

Dubnow, Simon.
    1927 Weltgeschichte des Jüdischen Volkes. (World history of the Jewish people.) Vol. VI. Berlin.

Dubnow, Simon.
    1928 Weltgeschichte des Jüdischen Volkes. (World history of the Jewish people.) Vol. VII. Berlin.

Dünner, J. H.
    1902 Leerredenen gedurende het Zomersemester 5661-62. (Sermons during the Summer Semester 5661-62.) Amsterdam.

Ejges, S.
    1930 Das Geld im Talmud. Versuch einer systematischen Darstellung der wirtschaftlichen Geldtheorie und -praxis nach talmudischen Quellen. (Money in the Talmud. An attempt at a systematic description of business finance theory and practice from Talmudic sources.) Wilna.

Feber, G. H. A.
    1940 De criminaliteit onder de Katholieken in Nederland. (Criminality among the Catholics in The Netherlands.) The Hague.

Gerth, H. H. & Mills, C. Wright.
    1966 From Max Weber: Essays in Sociology. New York.

Gerzon, Ed.
    1925 De Joden en de volkswelvaart in Nederland. (Jews and national prosperity in The Netherlands.) In: Gedenkboek Centraal Blad voor Israelieten in Nederland. Amsterdam. pp 44-45.

Hill, Michael.
    1973 A Sociology of Religion. London.

Hoffmann, M.
   1910 Der Geldhandel der deutschen Juden während des Mittelalters bis zum Jahre 1350. (Banking of the German Jews during the Middle Ages up to 1350.) Leipzig.

S.K.
   1925 Amsterdamsche Jodenhandel. (Jewish trade in Amsterdam.) In: Gedenkboek Centraal Blad voor Israelieten in Nederland. Amsterdam. pp 53-56.

Kitsur Shulchan 'Aruch. (Code of Jewish Law.)

Kruijt, J. P.
   1968 Mentaliteitsverschillen in ons volk i.v.m. godsdienstige verschillen. (Differences in attitude among the Dutch people in relation to religious differences.) In: Zoeklicht en kompas. Assen. pp 28-71.

Lemmen, M. M. W.
   1977 De godsdienstsociologie van Max Weber. (Max Weber's sociology of religion.) Nijmegen.

Meijer, J.
   1949 Hugo de Groot: Remonstrantie nopende de ordre dije in de landen van Hollandt ende Westvrieslandt dijent gestelt op de Joden. (Hugo de Groot: Remonstrance concerning the need to create order among the Jews in Holland and West Friesland.) Amsterdam.

Meijers, L. D.
   1974 De Reb Arrelech Chassidiem van Mea Sheariem. (The Reb Arrelech Chassidim of Mea Shearim.) Amsterdam. (Free University research report; publication in preparation.)
   1935 Outlines of the social and communal work of Chabad-Lubavitch. New York. (Anonymous.)

Palache, J. L.
   1954 Inleiding in de Talmoed. (Introduction in the Talmud.) Haarlem.

De Quiros, F. T. Bernaldo.
   1958 The Spanish Jews. Madrid.

Da Silva Rosa, J. S.
   1925 Geschiedenis der Portugeesche Joden te Amsterdam 1593-1925. (History of the Portuguese Jews in Amsterdam 1593-1925.) Amsterdam.

Sombart, Werner.
   1911 Die Juden und das Wirtschaftsleben. (The Jews and business life.) Leipzig.

Tal, J.
   1930 Chewro-Voordrachten gehouden in de Chewras Misjne Tora te Utrecht in den winter van 5689 (1928-'29). (Chewro Discourses held in the Chewras Mishne Tora at Utrecht in the winter of 5689; 1928-'29.) Utrecht.

Tal, T.
1881 Een blik in Talmoed en Evangelie. Tevens mijn laatste woord aan Prof. Oort in deze zaak. (A look into the Talmud and the Gospels. Also my final comment about this matter for Prof. Oort.) Amsterdam.

Tal, T.
1898 Oranjebloesems, uit de Gedenkbladen van Neerlands Israel. (Orange blossoms, memories of Dutch Israel.) Amsterdam.

Tennekes, J.
1969 De "Oud-Gereformeerden". (The "Old Dutch-Reformed".) Mens en Maatschappij 44: 365-385,

Weber, Max.
1958 The Protestant ethic and the spirit of capitalism. New York.

Weber, Max.
1960 Ancient Judaism. Clencoe (Ill.).

Weber, Max.
1964 The religion of China. Confucianism and Taoism. New York.

Weber, Max.
1965 The sociology of religion. London.

Weber, Max.
1967 The religion of India. New York.

Zwarts, Jac.
1922 Portugeesche Joden te Maarssen en Maarsseveen in de 17e eeuw. (Portuguese Jews in Maarssen and Maarsseveen in the 17th century.) n.p.